Terror
on
The High Seas

<u>Important Information</u>

The photos given inside the book have been given by the author. The publisher tried best to make them more visible but due to non-availability of good originals, the best possible have been done. The publisher is not responsible for the quality of photos which is deeply regretted.

Terror

on
The High Seas

Aditya Bakshi
Mercantile Marine Officer

Manas Publications
New Delhi-110002 (INDIA)

MANAS PUBLICATIONS

(Publishers, Distributors, Importers & Exporters)
4858, Prahlad Street,
24, Ansari Road, Darya Ganj,
New Delhi - 110 002 (INDIA)
Ph.: 23260783, 23265523 (O); 27131660
Fax: 011-23272766
E-mail: manaspublications@vsnl.com
Web site: www.manaspublications.com

First Published 2004

ISBN 81-7049-160-6
Rs 495/-

Typeset at
Manas Publications

Printed in India at
Nice Printing Press
and Published by Mrs Suman Lata for
Manas Publications, 4858, Prahlad Street,
24, Ansari Road, Darya Ganj,
New Delhi - 110 002 (INDIA)

Dedicated

To

**Mom and Dad, for encouraging me to read
and for listening patiently to the many stories that I
scrawled in my boyhood years. Some things never
change.**

Acknowledgements

The subject of "Terror on the High Seas", is one that must exercise the minds of all Merchant Navy officers and all those involved with Maritime Trade and Security. This book has entailed many months of research in various libraries and on the internet.

I am grateful to my father, Brigadier G D Bakshi SM, VSM, who encouraged me to write this book and shared with me some of his considerable hands on experiences in Counter Terrorist operations in J&K and Punjab. He gave me a clear understanding of terrorist activities, organisations and modus operandi on land. I have tried to extrapolate them to the Sea. I am grateful to my mother Suneeta and my sister Purnima for typing and editing the drafts of this book and for their constant encouragement and support. I am also grateful to my friends Hemant Vats and Swati Sirpaul for assistance in research on the Internet and in formating the data and preparing the graphs and illustrations. I must also place on record my gratitude to Mr Vivek Garg of the Manas Publications who encouraged me to write on this topical issue and to my grandparents Dr and Mrs S P Bakshi, Smt. Shakuntala Datta and my friend Nikhil Varma and my friend at sea, Pankaj Arya, and above all Mr Yogendra Ghatori for their suggestions and support.

I would also like to place on record my gratitude to Captain Commodore Surinder Mohan for being my mentor and guide in my seafaring career.

Aditya Bakshi

"Au regne grand du grand regine regant......

Port demoly net a fons iour ferain"

(In the kingdom of the great one.......
the Port Demolished, the ship at the Bottom,
a Severe Day)

Nostradamus

Contents

Prologue

The Trajectory of Terror

Backdrop

9/11 was a defining moment in world history. Suicide terrorists hijacked four American Airliners that were laden with high octane aviation fuel. They turned them into human guided cruise missiles that slammed into the Twin Towers of the World Trade Center in New York and completely incinerated this magnificent symbol of Western Capitalism.

They had leveraged the civilian air liner resources and aviation fuel of America itself to launch a horrendous attack on the Continental United States. It was the first time in 300 years that the Continental United States itself had been struck so savagely. Pearl Harbour (07 Dec 1941) had been another such defining moment in American history. An armada of six Japanese aircraft carriers had struck the American air base at Hawaii Islands in the Pacific and destroyed almost the entire American fleet anchored there. The massive US Air Base was left burning and over 2390 Americans were killed.[1]

The Japanese fleet and air aviation assets, however, had managed to target just an outlying air base of America. They had not been able to come anywhere close to the Continental United States itself. The American homeland had remained safe and secure through both the World Wars and the Cold War. Then that rubicon was crossed in one horrific day.

Terror Tuesday

To grasp the full import of how terror transformed our world at the very outset of the 21st century, let us recount the events of that Apocalyptic day in some more detail. Between 0758 Hrs and 0938 Hrs on 11 Sep 2001, a group of 19 terrorists (most of them Saudi Egyptian and Omani nationals) had used simple knives to hijack four American commercial jet airliners (Two Boeing 757 and two Boeing 767 liners).[2] They had very methodically and calculatingly chosen long distance flights that were heavily laden with highly inflammable aviation fuel.

Now came the macabre twist to the standard hijacking scenarios. Some of the hijackers (led by Ata Mohammed) had trained for months in piloting aircraft in flying schools in Florida and elsewhere. These suicide pilots now smashed these aviation fuel laden aircraft into the targets carefully selected for their symbolism[3].

The terrorists had leveraged upon the resource of the American commercial jet liners to turn them into lethal human guided missiles. These were simple tactical terrorist actions that had a massive strategic impact. These critical 120 minutes transformed world history. One by one, two successive jet airliners smashed into the Twin Towers of the WTC. Then the Pentagon, the very heart of American military power was struck viciously. Colossal damage was caused to life and property. The worst moments came when a fourth hijacked Airliner began to head ominously for the White House in Washington DC. There was complete panic and pandemonium in the White House. Apparently, the

Security Services asked all the staff to run for safety - to flee the White House. The US Air Force was apparently asked to shoot the civilian air liner down. The White House was presumably saved by the heroic resistance put up by the passengers of the doomed plane, which caused it to crash well away from its projected target[4].

A car bomb exploded in front of the US State Department. The United States reeled under these successive shocks. The US Government realised that it was under a meticulously planned and well co-ordinated attack. The whole of America was seized by a wave of panic and fear. All air line flights were grounded for four days and foreign airliners turned back from American airspace. This was the first time in history that America was forced to completely close its airspace to all commercial traffic for over 48 hours[5].

The American President and key officials were flown from one secret location to another, even as the world watched, mesmerised the horror of the crumbling of the 110 storey Twin Towers in a cloud of dust and ash. Reality TV projected this horror into every drawing room across the globe. It had captured one of the Jet liners smashing into the second tower. The aviation fuel caused a huge fire ball in the center of the sky scraper. The intense heat generated by the burning of the high octane fuel melted the steel support structures and brought them crashing down in a cascade of concrete, even as the terrified US citizens ran in panic in the streets below to avoid the collapsing infernos.

Terror Tuesday constitutes the zenith of terror, its high water mark which proved counter productive for the terrorists themselves. After careful and methodical preparation, the US struck back forcefully. Operation

"Enduring Freedom", was launched to destroy the Taliban regime and smoke out Osama bin Laden and his Al Qaida thugs from the caves in that barren land. The campaign was launched in two phases.

In the first phase, American Special Forces vectored in massive Air strikes with B-2 and B-52 strategic bombers and F-16 and F-18 fighter bombers. Massive Daisy cutter bombs, thermo baric bombs and Joint Direct Attack Munitions were launched to stun and pulverize the Taliban. The Northern Alliance then merely mopped up and occupied Kabul and the whole of Northern Afghanistan in less than a fortnight.[6]

In the second phase, US ground troops (the 101 Air Borne division and the US 10 Infantry Division) closely supported by Air Power and Afghan troops attacked Al Qaida bases in South Western Afghanistan[7]. The Taliban and their Al Qaida guests suffered an ignomimous military rout.

However, as many senior Intelligence operatives pointed out, the Al Qaida was temporarily down but not out. Its global terror network was severely disrupted and left leaderless and unco-ordinated, but it had thereby become more nebulous and diffuse. It now existed in the minds of men and could regroup and strike again in diverse ways and different forms. Terror Tuesday had transformed the world forever.

Mega Terror

What happened to the American Civil Aviation Industry is instructive. Terror Tuesday caused a loss of 70 billion dollars to the American exchequer which had to rehabilitate the reeling American Civil Aviation Industry and bail out a terrified insurance sector.

Alan Hevisi, the New York city Comptroller estimated the overall damage cost at a horrendous 105 billion dollars. More than 115,000 jobs were lost. Six top US Airlines alone laid off 85,000 workers while Boeing cut its work force by some 20 to 30,000 men. US economists had then predicted a final lay off figure of 500,000 workers. The critical consumer confidence Index fell from 91.5 points in Aug 2001 to 81.8 points in September. Wall street, Dow Jones Index slumped by more than 14% in the first week after the terror bombings.

Global vulnerability: The Merchant Marine

This book seeks to draw attention to a huge global vulnerability –a target system that could have an even more horrendous impact on the US and global economy than Terror Tuesday. UNCTAD (United Nations Conference on Trade and Development) estimates that 5.8 billion tons of goods were traded by sea in 2001. This accounts for over 80% of world trade by volume. The bulk of this trade is carried by 46,000 vessels serving nearly 4000 ports in the world[8].

Airliners have been the traditional target of terrorist groups since the Palestinian Diaspora. 9/11 has fully alerted the world to this threat and airports and the aviation industry have adopted stringent security measures.

A study by the Jaffee Center of Strategic Studies in Israel-had described terrorism as theatre. Through his tactical actions, the terrorist seeks to have a global impact via the media. The media is the force multiplier that enables him to influence a far larger audience than that available at the site of the terrorist incident. The theatre analogy means that target systems and modes of attack have to be varied constantly, otherwise they tend to loose their media value and psychological impact.

In its closing phase, the Palestinian Terrorist Movement had also effected the switch from hijacking airliners to hijacking ocean going ships with the hijack of the 'Achille Lauro' —an Italian cruise liner in 1985.

Today, there are a host of intelligence leads and inputs which are warning us of a clear and impending danger. Terror is likely to transit to the high seas. The next set of dramatic terrorist attacks will in all probability occur on the worlds merchant marine fleet. It is imperative that the shipping Industry transits to a crisis mode in an anticipatory reflex that must be in place well before these terrorist strikes start to happen.

Al Qaida: Current Status

The Al Qaida terrorist networks hierarchical structure has been severely disrupted by the US invasion of Afghanistan. There is however little ground for complacency. These terrorist networks have simply been displaced and dispersed but they have not been destroyed. In fact they have become much more amorphous and diffuse and to that extent more difficult to detect and attack. They are truly stateless actors. They can launch attacks from countries where they do not belong. What is critical to note is the fact that in the year 1998, Osama Bin Laden had formed the International Islamic Front (IIF). This was created much on the lines on which an International Communist Front had operated in the heydey of Communism. This affiliated most of the Islamic Terrorist Groups operating world wide. It specifically included organisations in Pakistan, Afghanistan, Central Asian Republics, Indonesia, Philipines, Egypt, Yemen and Algeria.

Today, though the Al Qaida and Taliban have been seriously disrupted, the affiliated groups like the Abu Syaff and Free Acheh Movement are very much active and thriving and have staged a number of bomb blasts. The recent terror bombings of Bali and Madrid have clearly highlighted the recuperative powers of the global terror network. The global war against terrorism is far from over[9]. The most worrisome dimension is the slowly emerging linkage between such non-state actors and weapons of mass destruction (WMD).

- Stefan Leader, a terrorism specialist with Eagle Research Group Inc (Arlington USA), highlighted this WMD trail in his article in the Janes Intelligence Review of June 1999. He pointed out that in Aug 1996 Bin Laden had declared war against the USA. Through a series of Fatwas issued in 1996, 1998 and 1999 he had incited Muslims to declare *Jehad* against the USA.[10]

- As far back as in 1993, Mamdoud Mahmud Salim (alias Abu Hijarat Iraqi–a close associate of Bin Laden) had tried to purchase highly enriched Uranium.[11]

- The Jehadi terrorist may not be able to fabricate a suitcase nuclear bomb in the basement or backyard. However experts have highlighted that they could easily fabricate a dirty bomb or a Radiological Dispersal Device (RDD). The RDD is a conventional explosive with radioactive material attached to it. It has been speculated that terrorists could use commercially available radio active material such as Cesium 137 or Cobalt 60. These are highly radioactive materials used for medical and industrial purposes and are readily available.[12]

- Conventional Explosives could also be employed to spread powdered Anthrax – a relatively deadly biological agent.[13]

Apocalypse Now: The Fifth Horseman

Well over a decade ago, the best selling piece of fiction called "The Fifth Horseman", had outlined a spine chilling scenario of terrorists smuggling in a suitcase nuclear bomb into the USA. The route chosen was via a container in a commercial container carrying ship. The "fifth horseman" being the mythical horseman who would bring about the Apocalypse or total destruction of the world. The fictive scenario had very precisely identified the huge vulnerability of the future, (well before the numerals 9/11 had embedded themselves so deep into the collective human consciousness.)

The Al Qaida is now slowly regrouping and reactivating itself. It has a vast choice of soft targets. And no nation in the world, not even America, can defend any target, anywhere and at anytime for any length of time. Where then are the Al Qaida strikes likely to come next?

The Most Penetrable Target Environment

One of the most easily penetrable and most vulnerable target environment for the terrorists today is on the high seas. There are huge fleets of some 46,000 unprotected and unsuspecting Merchant Ships and Tankers carrying oil or cargo or containers.[14] 16 million containers are moved around the world each year. Very few of them are subjected to any worth while scrutiny of the contents. Even if they are checked on the ports of embarkation, there is no way to ensure that these are not tampered with enroute[15]. 'The Fifth Horseman' of the Apocalypse had come to the coast of the United States ensconced in a container. There is therefore a clear and pressing danger.

Then there are the Ocean liners carrying the passengers that constitute a huge vulnerability. The 9/11 terrorists had hijacked air liners and turned them into human guided cruise missiles. Terrorists today could vary that macabre theme and hijack massive oil tankers and turn them into battering rams or huge human guided torpedoes that could smash into the Jetties of the major ports of the world and wreak havoc. The possibilities and variations of the theme of mega terror on the sea are numberless. The terrorists could pick and choose their targets with ridiculous ease. 85 percent of the global trade moves by sea routes on the merchant fleets. Some 4000 ports are the hub centers of global commerce and the ends of energy lifelines[16]. The sea lanes are the life lines of the global economy. How well protected are these arteries? The answer to this question is a chilling prospect of a disaster simply waiting to happen.

The shipping industry today has huge vulnerabilities like piracy, maritime crime, Flags of convenience, and poor or non-existent scrutiny of container contents. At the sea ports, the security standards and access control is abysmally poor. The lack of accountability along the whole transport chain lends it extremely susceptible to organized terrorist attacks.

Flags of Convenience

Flags of convenience is one example of an endemic liability that could facilitate such attacks[17]. Just consider this amazing scenario. The worlds largest merchant shipping fleets ostensibly belong on paper to three little known countries:-

- Bahamas
- Panama
- Liberia

Liberia however is not so "little known". It was recently in the headlines for a raging civil war, genocide and mayhem. Its former President, Charles Taylor, has variously been called an international criminal and his deputy Foday Sanko, has been busy sacking the diamond mines of neighbouring Sierra Leone.

On paper a virtual rogue country and failed state like Liberia actually owns a merchant fleet of 1557 ships! The ships of course are registered on paper only. Andrew Lenington of the National Union of Maritime Aviators and Shipping Transport Officers of the USA pointed out that "this helps them to avoid taxes and line the pockets of corrupt port officials". This practice of Flags of Convenience could open up significant vulnerabilities that terrorists could easily exploit.

The Coming Convergence of Piracy and Terrorism

What lends far greater credibility to these doom scenarios is the likely convergence of the phenomena of piracy and terrorism. Piracy was supposed to be a historical anachronism from the Middle Ages. When the UN Conference of the Laws of the Seas was carrying out its deliberations in the 1970s, it generally glossed over the subject of piracy as a relic of history. Surprisingly the phenomena of piracy began to resurface soon thereafter in the late 1980s and 1990s. There has been a disturbing rise in the number of incidents of piracy since then and the trend is growing. What is most disturbing is a geographic and phenomenal convergence of the areas of rising Muslim fundamentalism with the onset of piracy. As of now the two phenomena are not yet linked visibly but the linkages, in all probability are already well in place. The prime areas of rising piracy are in South East Asia (off the thousands of Islands in Indonesia and Philippines); off the Coasts of South Asia (India's Andaman chain of islands and off Sri Lanka and Bangladesh) and in the Coastal regions of West Africa.

Most of these areas have huge Muslim populations. For the last more than a decade, the Al Qaida has assiduously been trying to cultivate fanatic cells amongst the Muslim populations of Indonesia and the Philippines. There is a virulent fundamentalist Muslim movement currently active in Acheh in Indonesia. Abu Sayaff is becoming a local Bin Laden clone in the Philippines and has been held responsible for bomb attacks in Bali. If it is any comfort, a large proportion of crews for the worlds merchant fleet are recruited from Indonesia and the Philippines. The possibility of terrorists infiltrating these crews are inordinately high. The possibility of terrorists hijacking ships off the Indonesian or Philippines coast could be even higher. Infact off Indonesia GAM has utilised existing piracy networks to hijack ships and demand ransom from owners to secure release of ship or crew.

Al Qaida is reported to have a Phantom Fleet of some 20 ships. One of these ships reportedly supplied the explosives used for the bomb blasts in Kenya. These operate under Flags of Convenience of Bahamas, Liberia and the Isles of Mann.

The Threat Materialises

The possibility of mega terrorist strikes on the high seas is no longer a matter of pure conjecture or the subject of fictive scenarios by imaginative writers. These acts are now a reality. As far back as 1961, political insurgents had attacked the Portuguese ship Santa Maria. The most famous sea hijack occurred in Oct 1985 when the Palestinian terrorists hijacked the Italian cruise liner *"Achille Lauro."* On 11 July 1988, terrorists of the Abu Nidal Group attacked the Greek Cruise Ferry named *City of Poros*. They killed 9 passengers and wounded over a hundred.

On 12th Oct 2000 the US Navy Destroyer *USS Cole* was attacked by Yemeni Terrorists in Aden harbour. Just two years later, virtually in the same area, the French Oil

Tanker *MT Limburg* was struck by a fiber glass boat carrying a huge charge of explosives. It blew an 8 meter diameter hole in the ships star board flank. The same Yemeni terrorist outfit claimed responsibility for the attack.

The Japanese vessel *Alondra Rainbow* was hijacked off Jakarta by Indonesian pirates. Days later, it was spotted by an alert Indian Master. Its name had been painted over. A Dornier air craft of the Indian Coast Guard was sent to track it. Ultimately, it was captured by two Indian Navy Missile boats off the coast of Tuticorin. The Japanese were deeply grateful for this rescue. It is well known that during the US campaign against Afghanistan, on American request, Indian Navy warships patrolled the straits of Malacca and escorted American logistics ships through these pirate/terrorist infested waters. Intelligence reports indicate that photographs of oil tankers and other ships transiting through these straits have been recovered in Al Qaida camps in Afghanistan. These clearly indicate the terrorists interest in this highly penetrable target environment. The worlds merchant marine ships, oil tankers and ports are under clear threat and already in the cross hairs of terrorist groups. The employment of RDD by the terrorist is no longer a question of "if" but "when and where".

Security Initiatives

A concerted and co-ordinated terrorist strike against ports and merchant ships could prove to be catastrophic for the global economy. A series of tactical strikes could have a huge regional and global impact. In war game simulations, B. Alan Hamilton of Washington DC, analysed the effects of dirty (RDD) bombs on American ports. He concluded that such a strike could close major American ports for a week with a direct loss to the US economy amounting to

58 billion dollars.[18] The pay offs of such strikes are huge. No wonder then that the US Transportation Security Agency has allocated 92.3 million dollars grants to 51 ports located throughout America in Jul 2002. This is part of a massive drive to ensure/improve:

- Facility Access Control
- Physical Security of Ports
- Cargo Security
- Passenger Security

Amending the SOLAS Convention: The ISPS Code

Formerly security aspects on sea were covered by the International Convention on the Security of Life at Sea (SOLAS) which was promulgated in 1974. As a result of the traumatic events of 9/11 these were found wholly inadequate to deal with piracy and terrorism. The International Maritime Organisation (IMO) decided in Nov 2001 to develop new measures relating to the security of ships and port facilities. After much spadework, the Diplomatic Conference on Maritime Security took place in London from 09-13 Dec' 2002. This Conference adopted amendments to the existing SOLAS Convention which specifically deal with the new threats. It decided to install Automatic Identification Systems (AIS) on all ships and adopted new Regulations for marking of ship Identification numbers and carriage of a Continuous Synoptic Record. It provided detailed guidelines for Ship and Port Security Plans and Duties of officials (ship/port security officers and company security officers). This has been the first meaningful and global initiative to deal with the problem of piracy and terrorism on the high seas. The ISPS (The International Code for the Security of Ships and Port Facilities) Code is the new Bible for maritime security issues.

US Customs Container Security Initiative

Each year more than 16 million containers arrive in the USA by ship, rail and road. In the year 2001 the US customs processed more than 214,000 vessels and 5.7 million containers. The US Customs and Coast Guard and Homeland Security officials are clearly taking the doomsday scenario of the fifth Horseman materialising in a cargo container very seriously. The seaman credential issue is also being tackled on a war footing. The New International Convention on Verifiable Seamen's Identification was completed by June 2003. The International Ship and Port Security code has been formulated and was adopted by the Conference on maritime security held from 09-13 Dec 2002 and is to come into force in 2004. CTPAT and other measures are also worthy of note. Department of Homeland Security in USA has its own agenda and set of specific initatives.

The Indian Angle

India has a total of 12 major and 184 minor ports. About 85% of India's overseas trade of 224 million tons between 1999-2000 was carried by sea. As of 01 Aug 2001, the total number of Indian merchant ships was 554 with approximately 7 million gross registered tonnage. Indian officers and crews serve with many international shipping lines. Indian Shipping contributed over Rs 3500 crores in foreign exchange in 1990-2000.[19]

Israel and India rank next only to the USA as a designated target of terrorists. Terrorist and insurgent movements have long been carrying out gun running in our coastal areas and in 1993 there were huge bomb blasts in the port city of Mumbai. Another series of bomb blasts shook the Indian Metropolis of Mumbai in 2003.

The threat is most clear and palpable. We can not afford to adopt a reactive mode which enables the terrorists to mount high profile strikes before we put in place our response/ defensive measures. We must anticipate the threat and act well in time to head it off. Attacks on merchant ships and port facilities are no longer a question of if – but only when and where. To be forewarned is to be forearmed. This book seeks to analyse the threat profile and take stock of the possible counter measures. It outlines credible future terrorist strike scenarios and analyses how technology and innovativeness can provide us viable solutions that can head off this threat. The risks involved in prevarication are simply too colossal to contemplate.

Notes

1. Ashok Malik and Lavina Melwani "Sixty minutes", Article in *India Today* 24 Sep 2001 issue.

2. *Ibid.*

3. *Ibid.*

4. *Ibid.*

5. Evan Thomas et al. " The Road to 11 September" Article in *News Week* 01 Oct 2001 issue.

6. Doyle Mc Manus. Report Published in the *Times of India* dated 10 Oct 2001.

7. Thomas. E. Ricks. Report published in the *Times of India* dated 10 Oct 2001.

8. UNCTAD Report cited in US *Maritime Transport Committee Report,* Jul 2003 prepared for Organisation for Economic Cooperation and Development.

9. AK Verma " Identifying the Nature of Current Terrorisim : What Its Containment Requires. *Indian Defence Review* Vol 18 (i) dated Jan-Mar 2003.

10. Stefan Leader. "Osama Bin Laden's Quest for Weapons of Mass Destruaction "*Janes Intelligence Review.* Jun 1999 issue. Pp 34

11. *Ibid.*

12. *Ibid.*

13. *Ibid.*

14. US Maritime Committee Report. *See* Note 8.

15. *Ibid.*

16. *Ibid.*

17. *Ibid.*

18. B Alan Hamilton, Washington DC.

19. Rahul Roy Choudhury. "India's Maritime Security" *Knowledge World* New Delhi, Jun 2000, pp 10.

◀1▶

Fateful Friday

Predicting Terror Scenarios: Facts, Fiction and Nostradamus

Some days go down in collective human memory. They embed themselves in our consciousness. Terror Tuesday (or 9/11) was one such day. Osama Bin Laden had said that on that day America would know fear and tremble. His fanatical band of followers had managed to do what even great maritime and military powers like Japan and Germany had failed to do in the World Wars. They had struck the Continental United States itself, turning her Jetliners into human guided cruise missiles. They had used her high octane aviation fuel to burn down the Twin Towers, to target the Pentagon and were aiming at the White House itself when they were foiled. Terror Tuesday was a nightmare. But Fateful Friday was far, far worse. What happened on fateful Friday was a terrible Apocalypse. It was the worst nightmare of Post Industrial Civilisation.

The Fifth Horseman of the Apocalypse had descended not from the Air or the Clouds, he had come from the Sea in a container. On that day the port was demolished and as Nostradamus had predicted, ships lay at the bottom of the world's busiest waterway.

D-Day minus One, Thursday 05 July 2006

Enroute to Baltimore

Friday, Holy 'Jumma' was just a day away. The day most sacred to the Muslims. The day on which millions of followers of the world's largest growing religion offer prayers together in Mosques all around the globe. A day of religious fervor, wish fulfilment, well being and charity.

Friday, the 06th of Jul 2006 was unfortunately about to be a day misused by the self styled *Jehadis*. *Jehad*, the so called Holy war which now concentrated largely on the killing of innocent people through secretive and organized terror attacks. Whether such acts actually befitted the adage of '*Jehad*' was a debate, but it didn't matter. It didn't matter to the terror networks operating with the sole aim of undermining the worlds setup and economies.

And it didn't matter to Abu Hassan.

For all Abu Hassan concentrated upon was the Prime Objective. The Prime Objective of ensuring the transportation of, and the 'blooming of' the 'Holy Fire' box. Abu Hassan's mind went blank at times. He recounted how they had performed his "*janaza*", his funeral ceremony even as he watched. The buzzing intonations of the funeral chants still murmured in his mind. They were performing his last rites even as he lived and breathed. They buried the empty casket. They piled the earth and mud on it. He was witnessing his own burial. He was hearing his own funeral lament. He was now a living dead. He was no ordinary mortal any more. He was a Ghazi devoted to the execution of his murderous mission.

Holy Friday, and a day before. Yes, Thursday mattered too. For that was the day the 6,600 TEU container carrying capacity vessel, *M.V. Seuying Kim* was due to dock into the bustling harbour of Baltimore, a major U.S port.

It had been a long voyage for the *M.V. Seuying Kim*. It had been an even longer voyage for Abu Hassan.

A few days ago, the seals of a container in a port warehouse were carefully removed by taking out the handles of the container door along with the rivets. The workers within the warehouse had tipped off the thieves when the paperwork for the containers had been done. The personnel manning the gate also assisted the thieves who drove in with a pickup truck full of material. The workers in the compound were told that the objective was to steal some expensive cargo in the containers and that since the ports paperwork was largely done, the claim for the stolen cargo would fall on the ship's crew. The workers and security personnel who had become familiar with the perpetrators were rewarded handsomely. So handsomely, that they wondered as to what the cargo being stolen from the containers would fetch the pilfering group.

No one paid attention to a container which seemed to house nothing except a makeshift bed, bathroom and was now stocked with a laptop, cellular phone, food supplies and a black suitcase which was carefully placed. Neither did anybody notice the dark shadow lurking in the confines of the container. The containers were carefully resealed and the thieving party tipped the workers and then drove out of the compound...all except one.

Abu Hassan was now ensconced in a container whose seal number and identification were checked against a manifest prior to loading – all was seemingly in order. All was seemingly in order – for Abu Hassan and his group, who had managed to successfully plant him and his lethal luggage on a container carrying vessel bound for the U.S.A.

Throughout the long voyage Hassan had stayed in the container, clutching the contoured container walls, praying vehemently as the stormy seas caused the vessel to roll and pitch violently.

Right after midnight on Wednesday, his cell phone, which he had calculatingly switched on a few hours earlier, caught a signal and lit up. The coast was near, he inferred and let out a sigh of relief. He had successfully survived so far against odds including possible cutting loose of his container in the storm, but his mission was not over yet. It was far from it. Yet, as every moment passed, he was getting nearer and nearer to his destination and his target.

He opened his laptop Computer and hooked it to the Internet. He down-loaded a series of sizzling pornographic pictures –explicit and lurid. Abu Hasan, however, was not easing his sexual frustrations in that container with visual fantasies. He began to enlarge a dot in one of the pornographic images. It contained a coded message. He enlarged it further till it filled the whole screen. "Hope you have the flowers-and that all is well. May they bloom in full splendour on Friday upon your arrival".

On Thursday he could feel the vessel's motion slowing down and finally coming to a standstill. He down-loaded another message "Is it time yet?" he inquired. He was answered in the negative. His vessel had berthed and his container would be discharged soon.

"Remember"' he was told, "In case, the holy tomb of waters is opened by the 'kafirs' before it's time, it is upto you, the chosen one, the one who is 'shaheed' already and whose procession would be witnessed by the world, to let the flowers bloom immediately".

He understood. He looked at the black suitcase in front of him. In case of interception or a premature discovery of his lethal plans, he was to set off his weapon straightaway. He had made it to the port. It was only a matter of time.

A few hours later, he heard a clatter on the roof of his container. He clutched the suitcase in apprehension. The container shook, and he opened his suitcase, hysterically. His hands trembled as he took two wires of a trigger mechanism and stared wide eyed at the container door, perspiring profusely.

His container was picked up by a gantry crane and transferred from the vessel into the container berth, even as an inquisitive Deck Cadet questioned his Chief Officer, who answered, "Yes these operations are fast, container ships hardly stay in port more than a couple of days.

"It's down to a few hours in some – still better than a Car Carrier I was on, we did nine ports in a week – and even discharged a lone single car at Tema in the West Coast of Africa.

"About these containers ? Well I guess they'll lie in the docks till the customs inspect them in a few days, it's obviously not possible for us to do so. We discharge them by the hundreds in a day, you see".

D-Day minus one, on board *M.T. Kunar Viking*

Enroute to London

ETA Friday 0400 Hrs Local Time, This was the calculation of the Second Mate onboard *M.T. Kunar Viking* a few days ago—proceeding after bunkering at Tarifa Point, Gibraltar to Shetland Isles off U.K. He had just finished all the preliminary paperwork and called the Captain for review of the passage plan.

"That's the estimated time of arrival at the pilot station, if she does 15 knots", he told Hans Janiken – a tall Swede with a ruddy complexion – the Captain of one of the largest tankers in the world.

Hans studied the passage plan and then the charts – it looked like another routine voyage, except that – as he was soon going to find out – it wasn't.

He surveyed the traffic situation and then decided to retire. He confirmed with the bridge team that they were fit to take on the watch and had had their coffee. The helmsman didn't reply.

He repeated his query to Chiraz Memud - a Muslim Filipino from Mendanao. Hans stared at the helmsman who ignored him completely. The Second Mate intervened, labeling Memud a shy but diligent worker and expressed his confidence in his ability to keep a watch.

"Well, make sure he doesn't feel shy of repeating the helm orders." Hans said, after a pause, as he went down from the bridge to his cabin. He made a mental note to keep an eye on Memud, since he had also found him staying aloof from the rest of the crew. "Queer character"' he muttered to himself.

Shortly there after, he got a call from the second Mate on bridge. " It's a chopper sir, its been circling our vessel since the past few minutes."

The pipe smoking Swede came to the bridge and peered curiously at the medium sized cargo helicopter. It seemed to be descending lower and lower—the clatter of its huge rotors soon filled the air. Its downwash caused objects to fly off the deck of the Viking.

"Kunar Viking, Kunar Viking, Kunar Viking, this is Whisky Tango Charlie. Do you copy, over," the VHF radio transceiver crackled. Hans took the handset himself and replied back. It was the helicopter. It asked Hans to change over to a different VHF channel. Hans complied.

"Request that you have the starboard helipad area of the deck cleared for landing, over."

Hans paused, he was perplexed. Some of the crew who had been observing the chopper from the deck, assumed the chopper had all intentions of landing, and began clearing up the helipad, and folded the collapsible side railings.

"We have observed your vessel polluting these waters, we need to carry out an investigation."

"What?", Hans exclaimed, he let go off the handset and rushed to observe his vessels wake, he stooped over the bridge wings and peered at the ship side. There seemed to be no traces of oil. He hurried back to the wheel house and asked the chopper to confirm the identity of his vessel —the chopper reiterated its stand, and proclaimed that they had taken aerial photographs of the vessel polluting the seas. Hans was nonplussed—the liabilities and legal repercussions of an oil spill—an environmental disaster flashed in his mind.

"How can it be? Hope, the Chief Engineer's not upto something..! call the Chief Officer and confirm whether any operations were carried out not to my knowledge...any valve leaking...check!", he exclaimed.

He stared at the deck dumbfounded. The chopper which had been flying low all the time, had lowered a man awkwardly by winch onto the deck.

The third officer, who possessed a portable 'walkie-talkie' transceiver caught up with the man.

"He insists on being shown around the vessel, Sir" he reported.

"For God's sake what's going on?", Hans voice called over the radio's speaker. Hans couldn't think of what to do – the unexpected situation had him out of his wits.

"Just hold everything!" he called.

The man signaled to the helicopter by waving his arms and then disappeared into the accommodation. The chopper descended. It touched down on the deck. Instinctively, a few crew members rushed towards it with fire extinguishers – despite receiving no orders to that effect.

A stream of men in jet black overalls and masks donned on their faces emerged from the chopper. The leading man took position and aimed with his folded butt 'Kalashnikov'. He shot and killed the leading crewman who was approaching the helicopter. Then he shot the next crew member in his leg. The man screamed and fell down on the deck. The rest of the crew realising their vulnerability on a relatively flat tanker deck, lay down on deck with their hands on their heads.

"What the hell.....", the tall Swede Captain exclaimed. Another shot rang out towards the bridge and narrowly missed him.

He ducked and moved into the wheel-house taking cover under the chest high gunwale of the Bridge wing.

"Lock the doors of the Bridge! Quickly! Send a mayday on radio.... VHF, DSC everything" he screamed wildly. The Second Mate, trembling in fear began to move towards the GMDSS console.

"We'll do nothing of the sort."

The Second Officer froze. An astonished Hans whirled around to see Chiraz Memud wielding a long knife and advancing menacingly towards the second Mate, looking at the Swede with piercing eyes.

His suspicions were confirmed – he could not fathom the unbelievable situation yet.

"Memud, what's going on", he spluttered.

"You will see" Memud said firmly, "Now step aside ….."

The attackers meanwhile rushed upto the bridge like frenzied ants searching for prey. They barged at the door and burst in when Memud undid the latch. They fell upon the second Mate and beat him up mercilessly. One attacked Hans.

"For God's sake"' he choked out, "Why are you doing this?"

"For Iraq – for Amir Bin Laden and for all the insults your kind have heaped upon the faithful – you infidel dog" he hit him with his weapon.

Hans doubled over in pain.

A broad masked man, who appeared to be the leader picked him up by the scruff of his neck. "From now on you do what we say. OK ?"

The Swede could only nod in pain.

He walked over to the Filipino "Good job. Memud. I hope they were not able to radio anything." His walkie-talkie crackled. He brought it up to his ear. "They've secured the Engine Room". He announced.

"Good, tell the helicopter to get the material. The Black Box is to be brought to me".

He walked upto the chart-table and glanced at the charts. With a sweep of his hand he shoved them aside. Another masked man produced scrolls of papers which turned out to be maps.

"Take out charts pertaining to these maps, Captain and plot courses as marked.You will retain old voyage charts and send false position reports to your company and to the vessel reporting system you subscribe to. On Thursday you shall report Engine trouble and inform your intended destination that you can't make it".

Hans kept staring at the man.

"We shall pay London a little visit. If our hosts are a bit inquisitive, tell them we require repair facilities on an immediate basis – good old engine trouble again. Towards the end of our voyage we shall display not-under-command signals -- so that we are not bothered much ..... anyway, as for now, you shall lay courses and ensure your vessel follows them".

"That's implausible", Hans retorted, "They'll detect you, you can't pull this off ....tell you what? Why don't you just take the money and belongings and just ....." he couldn't finish his sentence. The leader had rammed the barrel of his AK-74 into his neck.

"One move from you Captain and we feed you and your crew to the sharks".

The helicopter which had taken off in the interim period, landed again. Two hooded men got down with a Box.

"Allahu Akbar"

The masked men shouted in frenzy. The box was received with gusto on the bridge subsequently, it was a RDD (Radiological Dispersal Device).

The helicopter made a few more short trips. Hans looked up from the charts time and time again with increasing apprehension, as the masked men got busy along the length of the vessel, opening radar domes of the tanks, which spewed off the inert gases of the large cargo tanks atmosphere.

The Inert Gas plant had been shut down as he could see from a gauge in the chart room. The atmosphere in the cargo tanks could now be more flammable. The helicopter's mysterious cargo was installed on what appeared to be – strategic points on the vessel-including the cargo tanks.

"These shouldn't be explosives" was all Hans could think. Panic grew in his heart as did the fervour in the leader's voice. "Inshallah, this Friday will be memorable", he exclaimed, boring down with fanatical eyes into Captain Hans Janiken's.

D-Day minus One, 05 July 2006, 2300 Hrs

The Malacca Straits

M. T. Priority was picking up provisions before venturing into the busy waters of the Malacca Strait. The supply tug was alongside and most of the crew were busy picking up provisions piled up on the deck by the ship's crane—and transferring them into the cold storage in the accommodation. The Second Mate on bridge decided to use the extra few hours to catch up on his chart correction.

Whilst in the chartroom he was unaware that at that very moment, a small craft, its specially streamlined fiberglass body undetected even by the radar, had pulled up alongside the stern of the huge VLCC. (Very Large Crude oil Carrier).

A grapnel hook was already entangled on the aft railings and a dark figure deftly made its way over a rope attached to it, leading to the small boat. He heaved himself over the railings and landed on the deck.

For a few moments into the dark night, he stood there, surveying the surroundings. There were mooring ropes still lying on the aft deck, the crew had decided against coiling and storing them in the after peak store, since they were expecting to berth in what they felt was a relatively short time. He picked up a thick nylon mooring rope and dragged it to the side. It was soon lowered against the Transom plate of the vessel—and more figures made their way up on to the vessel.

Even as the ship stocked, the dark silhouettes in the aft strained purposefully to pick up the last deadly deadweight—a cluster of guns—and soon, the small boat broke off in no time.

They clustered together and weapons were passed around. Quickly, the objectives were recited in hushed tones. The situation was re-reckoned and orders re-confirmed. With a final word, they broke off in different directions.

A group opened the dog leavers of an aft weather tight door and pushed it open. They took the ladder leading to the steering flat, right next to the Engine Room. They all knew the ships general arrangement plan like the back of their hands—a copy had been procured during the vessels dry dock in Dubai earlier.

Another group moved up the decks of the accommodation superstructure from the aft ladders, till they were right below the one housing the bridge. They sent messages to each other on portable radios. They were in position-but it wasn't their time yet. They had now to wait for the right moment.

While on the bridge, the VHF Transceiver happened to catch their radio conversations. A pre-occupied Second Mate cocked his head to listen to the unusual noise—but resumed his work when he couldn't comprehend the dialect and communications—assuming it to be 'interference caught from some nearby craft'.

D-Day: Fateful Friday

6 July 2006, 0100 Hrs Local Time, Baltimore Port USA

The container housing Abu Hasan and a Radiological Dispersal Device was moved by truck into a warehouse for inspection by customs. While it lay in the warehouse compound, Abu Hasan detonated the RDD - killing himself and spewing radioactive waste and radiation in a few miles radius. A sheet of orange flame surged through the harbour. Hundreds of direct casualties were incurred, with thousands of people in the vicinity exposed to the harmful and cancerous radioactive radiations. Baltimore had been well chosen. Baltimore is the centre for the huge Natural Gas trade. There were massive Natural Gas tanks that created gigantic secondary explosions.

It was like a nuclear strike. Sheets of searing orange flames engulfed the Port. Bellows of black smoke rose skywards. It was terrible. All major ports shut down in the U.S. for seven days—causing a direct loss to the American economy of 58 billion US Dollars. The Dow Jones Index fell 600 points in a single day. The price of Natural Gas escalated to hit the roof. It was an unprecedented catastrophe. A huge charge of conventional explosive had been attached to a large consignment of commercially available Cascum 137 and Cobalt 60. The radioactive materials were spewed all over the port city. Thousands had perished in the initial explosion. Thousands more were to die a slow lingering death due to the radiation. The Fifth Horseman of the Apocalypse had arrived. As it was foretold, he had come from the Sea.

D-Day:

1300 Hrs Local Time, Canary Wharf, London UK

Capt. Hans and his crew failed to stop a group of suicide hijackers from carrying out a hideously elaborate lethal mission—to use their huge vessel as the largest floating Torpedo ever, to deadly effect. Even the imploring of a Pakistani nationality Engineer fell on deaf ears. The *Kunar Viking* proceeded at full speed ahead with an assisting current of almost twenty knots. At this speed and momentum, it could ram through a jetty and keep going inshore for half a mile, with the sheer inertia of its huge hull.

On shore people watched in horror as the menacing giant lurched at them with full force. Minutes later, it sliced through them like a knife through butter—it seemed to go on and on, wreaking havoc on the constructions—leaving a trail of death and destruction in its wake.

Then they heard the terrific explosion. A million tons of crude oil caught fire and blazed like a massive volcano of light. More explosions followed causing a rain of fire and scalding oil. One of the explosions was another Radiological Dispersal Device that spewed Cobalt and Cesium all over the area and oil flaming river waters. Secondary explosions and fireballs started in adjacent buildings and cars and soon the whole dockyard was resounding with deafening explosions. Huge clouds of black smoke rose towards the sky in pillars of an ominous darkness. The region was contaminated with radioactive waste – it would remain unusable, to its full potential, for a hundred years. No rescue team could initially come anywhere close to the radioactive spill. It was a disaster of unprecedented magnitude. London was burning with radioactive fires.

D-Day

1900 Hrs Local Time, Kecil, Malacca Straits

M.T. Priority had been given a naval escort through the pirate infested waters of the Malacca Straits. Whilst in constricted waters with shallow depths the *Priority* was high-jacked by the intruders who had stowed away on the ship the night before. In a swift and precise move, control was taken of the *Priority's* bridge, at the same time ensuring total ignorance on part of the US naval warship escorting the tanker.

The naval warship was 'lured' to a strategic location and in an unexpected maneuver, the *Priority* rammed headlong into the US naval warship. The perpetrators managed to sink both vessels at a 'choke point' - stalling the whole traffic movement in these critical straits. Besides the loss of lives and the vessels, an oil spill occurred which nearly shut down the straits and took years to clean up.

The oil supply flow to major South East Asian economies was disrupted—causing a major economic crisis. 80 percent of Japans oil passed through these straits. So did a huge percentage of the oil supplies of China and the two Koreas. It was an unmitigated disaster.

The Horseman of the Fifth Apocalypse had struck from the Seas. His target was the human civilisation perse. His aim was to trigger a collapse of the global economy and gave a mortal blow to global trade. The hallmarks of this concerted and co-ordinated attack was its detailed and meticulous planning. The prime targets of the attack were the USA and UK in particular and the worlds sea borne trade in general. Radiological dispersal devices had been set off in Baltimore and London and a huge super oil tanker and an American warship had been sunk in the Straits of Malacca to block this critical choke point through which a huge proportion of the Middle Eastern oil for the Far Eastern economies of China, Japan and Korea used to pass. The post industrial global civilisation itself was under attack.

The most disturbing feature was the use of Weapons of Mass Destruction (WMD) by Non State Actors. A State can be deterred by threats of retaliation in kind. How do you deter a Non State Actor, with no name, no country and no State of his own? Just an empire in the minds of the fanatical and misguided, of those filled with silent rage and a huge persecution complex.

These fateful hours would go down as a Black Day in world history. Already that year the world had witnessed major maritime disasters.........But this was too horrendous to contemplate.

Earlier, a cruise vessel carrying 5000 passengers was sunk by terrorists. The terrorists also launched a suicide attack on an artificial airport built by Japan—extending 5 km into the sea—the largest man-made water structure then—destroying its foundations and crafts housed; again a sea borne vessel was used to inflict maximum damage.

A nuclear waste carrying ship was hijacked. Its contents misused. This list could go on—it could be tomorrow's reality.

However unlikely the above events seem to be in fiction, they are to be seen as realistic threats intimidating the shipping world today. All the above scenarios are possible, all of the above scenarios are also totally preventable. The following chapters seek to explore such threats—the trends and potentialities—and sketch a model of the current awareness and response strategies at all levels in the maritime world.

Notes

1. All Scenarios painted in this Chapter are purely fictive. Any resemblance to any actual person or vessel is purely coincidental. However, these hypothetical scenarios have been derived from a careful assesment of actual threats.

2. Philip Day. "Ship Piracy Stirs Terrorism Fears", report in *Wall Street Journal* of Jun 13-15, 2003. Inputs on Mallaca Straits Scenario based upon this report.

‹2›

Piracy and Maritime Crime
Precursor to Terrorism

Introduction

Let us now transit from the realm of hypothesis and conjecture to facts as they are on the ground and on the sea. The threat of terror on the high seas is no longer a matter of conjecture. A number of actual terror attacks have already taken place on the high seas. Many others are covered under the rubric of piracy. There are a host of Maritime crime issues which haunt the shipping industry today. The seriousness of the consequences of such activity rubs off the busy shoulders of a Herculean industry too engrossed in going about doing its business, an enterprise dictated by such factors as time sensitivity, liabilities and volumes of the trade. In the wake of 9/11 one of the most vulnerable environments that the terrorists could exploit with devastating effects, is the marine environment. At risk is the global trade, some 46,000 merchants ships and 4,000 ports. The risk is overwhelming, for a thriving enviroment of maritime crime, piracy and Flags of Convenience etc make the penetration of this marine environment ridiculously easy for the terrorists. We have to plug these serious loopholes of Maritime crime if we wish to avoid a mega terror strike at Sea.

Unfortunately, the statistics of maritime crime when compared against say, the number of ships that successfully plied from berth to berth, delivering their cargoes in good order, come across as a pittance to the casual onlooker. There is a tendency for these statistics to drown in the sheer volume of traffic and trade occurring in any chosen time period. Perhaps, this is the reason why most shipping players ignore the implications of such incidents and traditionally, the threat is perceived as "rare", "unfortunate" or "once unlucky", "asymmetrical" and worst, "won't happen to us - at least to the extent to affect us much."

Trade has not been really hampered by a 'few cases'. However today, there is a need to recognise the fact that the trend in maritime related crime is steadily increasing. Security related incidents are on the rise, the network is becoming more and more organised, evasive of detection, tactically innovative; there is an infiltration of guns and weapons in the nexus and as such these networks are now ripe for abuse by the big players in the terror game.

To review the crime statistics separately would bring home the gravity of the situation. The numbers are in themselves enough to spark concern. Maritime crime is a broad spectrum that spans such varied activities as piracy, cargo theft, illegal fishing, human and drug/ weapons smuggling, phantom / fraudulent shipping etc.

It is interesting to note that if a terrorist chooses to strike, he will make use of the entire existing spectrum—harvesting the varied crime setups, widely perceived as disconnected to cover up his tracks. The environment is one where any anti-shipping/ fraudulent activity is open to exploitation, with surprising ease by a terrorist cell.

There is a need to identify and establish maritime crime – especially piracy, in the context of marine terrorism. The ease with which these setups lend themselves to abuse, makes it a matter of rational inference, that today's 'small time' maritime crime, is tomorrow's 'major' terrorist network. Possible lack of opportunities to cause mayhem, beefed up security on land – and in an attempt to catch the world's attention in a novel way—and other such causative factors might set the stage for a 'migration of terrorism to the sea', with busy shipping lanes and major littoral states becoming the next prime targets of attack.

There is need to launch a comprehensive programme against maritime crime incorporating multilateral action, involving all the major maritime states.

The Revival of Piracy

The onset of the new Millennium was celebrated with great fervor around the globe. The world based sea-trade had experienced its 14th consecutive annual increase and the mood was upbeat. Even as little toddlers sported a black eye patch and skull depicting hats in historical theme parties, the general public never even imagined that this 'outdated' concept would reach a statistical peak in the year 2000. The phenomena of piracy is generally regarded as a relic of history. In the post industrial era, it could only be regarded as an anachronism. No wonder the protracted deliberations of The Law of The Sea Conference in the seventies spent little time or energy on this 'antiquated' issue. This was to be a costly omission. Surprisingly enough this 'ancient' crime began to resurface again in the eighties and in the nineties in an increasingly menacing way. The resurgence of this scourge of the seas acquired ominous proportions because today it has begun to be linked with the phenomena of global terrorism.

The International Maritime Bureau (IMB) defines piracy as, "An act of boarding or attempting to board any ship with the intent to commit theft or any other crime and with the intent or capability to use force in the furtherance of the act."[i] The International Maritime Bureau has adopted this definition as the majority of attacks against ships take place within the jurisdiction of states and as such do not satisfy the internationally agreed definition of piracy. This definition is somewhat contentious as it includes attempted and actual attacks and applies whether the victim ship is at anchor or berthed or at sea. To the mariner, whether he is technically a victim of piracy or terrorism, or any other crime, will not necessarily affect his response, as it is the nature of the act rather than its definition that matters.[ii]

In the modern context, piracy has three fundamental requirements for success[iii]

- Firstly, there needs to be a ready supply of ships to plunder where the potential rewards of piracy are worth the inherent risks of attaining them.

- Secondly, there is a requirement for an operating base that is either concealed or is in a lawless region or both.

- Thirdly, there needs to be a market, for a pirate cannot make a profit unless he finds a market. Moreover as long as the market exists, the pirate has every encouragement to pursue his trade.

The UNCLOS[iv] Conference that went into the issue of piracy merely reproduced the 1958 Geneva Convention on piracy in its Articles 100 to 108. Article 105 in fact stipulated that Piracy is an International crime. When the UNCLOS was being drafted, piracy was still an historical anachronism. It was from the eighties onwards that a sudden spurt was witnessed.

Initially, these incidents mostly took the form of thievery in which the culprits climbed aboard a merchant vessel by throwing grappling lines or jumping ladders, mainly in anchorages and then made away with the booty (often in connivance with the crew).

Disturbingly, with the above three conditions being satisfied with relative and tempting ease, the phenomena deteriorated to activities in which organized gangs, managed on shore, boarded ships, assaulted crew, even killed or set them adrift, sold off the cargoes illegally and plying under forged papers and fraudulent flags, exploited the vessel for nefarious purposes. These included all illegal activities imaginable including narcotics smuggling, clandestine movement of arms and weapons, illegal immigrants etc.

The new Millennium set a benchmark in the revived phenomenon of piracy.

In the year 2000 itself there were a total of 469 attacks on merchant vessels, which was more than double the average of the preceding decade (1991-2000) and these figures had increased by 56 % over those in 1999 (300). There were a total of 480 crew members subjected to violence of different types which was in excess of the decade average by 64%.

- 72 crew members were killed and 99 wounded.
- 8 ships were hijacked
- The maximum numbers of these incidents occurred in Indonesian waters (199).
- 75 such attacks (mostly thieving incidents) occurred in Indian waters.
- In 71 of these incidents guns were used.

Statistical/ Graphical Analysis

A statistical analysis of the piracy data furnished by the IMB is presented here in a series of graphs that trace the growth of this phenomena from a spurt in 1994 onwards.

Figure 1 charts the trends of piracy incidence at the global level from the year 1994 onwards. The graphs clearly indicate a sharp rise to 469 incidents as compared to 300. Despite the apparent reduction in the total number of

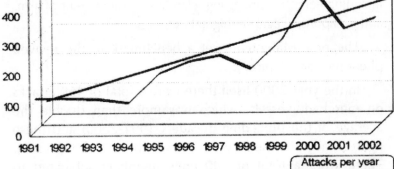

Piracy Attacks

reported cases of piracy in 2001, compared to the preceding year, the overall trend continues to rise with the last three years showing increase in incidents of piracy between 39% and 117% per year above the 11 year total

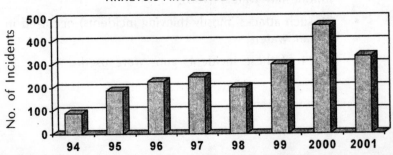

ANALYSIS : INCIDENCE OF PIRACY

average of 216. Not shown in the chart is the continuation of the trend with the year 2002 tally increasing to 370. Indonesia recorded the highest number of attack incidents in 2002. Piracy attacks in Bangladesh ranked second highest with 32 attacks and India was third with 18 attacks.

Regional Growth Trends

The following bar charts indicate regional growth trends. As can be seen from the graphs, piracy is a world wide phenomena. However, certain regions have had high affinity for infestation as is evident from the statistical data.

Piracy incidents have shown a distinct rise in areas with huge Muslim populations. Sections of these Muslim populations have been steadily coming under the influence of Fundamentalist organizations. Thus, the Free Aceh Movement in Indonesia has been escalating the levels of violence in that island nation. Abu Sayaaf has been a Bin Laden clone from the Philippines. The Al Qaida is active in Afghanistan, Pakistan, Yemen, Somalia and Singapore. The LTTE has been operating in the South Asian region. When we put this terrorist activity overlay on the global

REGIONAL INCIDENCE : SOUTH EAST ASIA

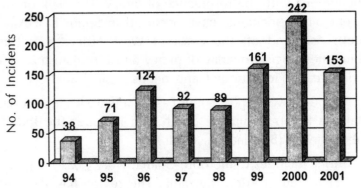

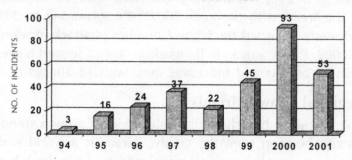

REGIONAL INCIDENCE : SOUTH ASIA

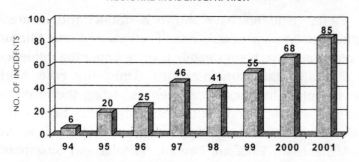

REGIONAL INCIDENCE: AFRICA

(Source : Data for all Bar Graphs based on IMO releases cited in Lt
Cdr. R.C. Browbick. "Piracy: Ancient Myth or Modern Reality". Naval
Review Feb 2003 Issue Vol 91. No 1)

map, we find a clear geographical convergence of this
phenomena with the resurgence of piracy. The bulk of the
recent piracy incidents have occurred in South East Asia,
South Asia and off the coast of West Africa. It is this
phenomenological overlay of piracy and terrorism that is a
serious cause for disquiet and needs critical analysis.

In the above graphs, South East Asia includes Indonesia,
Malacca Straits, Malaysia. South Asia includes the Indian
subcontinent (Bangladesh, India.)

Africa includes Cameroon, Ghana, Ivory Coast, Nigeria,
Red Sea, Gulf of Aden, Tanzania. This region has also had

the greatest rate of increase – the total for 2001 is above the decade average by 166% and up by 25% on the previous year figures. The waters off Somalia are among the most dangerous in the world. "The risk of attack on vessels staying close to the coastline from Somali armed militias has now increased from one of possibility to certainty," the IMB said in a news report in Feb 2003.

"Any vessel, not making a scheduled call in a Somali port, which slows down, or stops close to the Somali coast will be boarded by these gangs." They had extorted substantial sums from owners for the return of the vessel and crew. Since January 2002, there have been four high-profile hijackings of commercial vessels off Somalia. The attackers have sophisticated arms profile. For instance in Aug. 2001 *MV Maurice Ewig* was pursued by a small boat which the crew claimed was equipped with AK-47s and RPG-3s and had even fired a rocket on the vessel, which skid on the water but did not detonate.

The graphs indicate that the Far East region has witnessed a modest increase over the past 6 years.In South America, Brazil, Colombia, Dominican Republic, Ecuador and Guyana all showed a marked increase in attacks as per IMB Annual Report of 2002.

The incidents in Malacca Straits saw a remarkable drop in attacks to 17 in 2001 compared to 75 in the previous year. This is most likely due to increase in anti-piracy patrols conducted by the Royal Malaysian Marine Police and other relevant authorities. However, it is likely that the piracy got temporarily displaced and resurfaced in 2003. It is also likely that the pirates organised themselves into more organised crime networks as evidenced by the increased hijackings/ ransom incidents in the region that followed suit next year. This reinforces the need to launch a major operation to evict this nexus by its roots.

Violence Index Analyis

Bar charts in figure 1 and 2 indicate the year wise number of attacks with guns and knives. The rise in the use of the gun is a disturbing phenomena. The endemic loss of lives and the rising use of violence against passengers and crew has led some experts (like Vice Admiral Prem Vir Das,

ARMED WITH GUNS

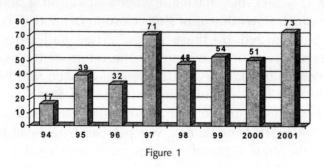

Figure 1

ARMED WITH KNIVES

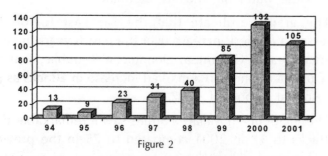

Figure 2

CREW TAKEN HOSTAGE

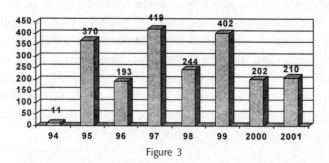

Figure 3

former Flag Officer Commanding-in-Chief of the Indian Navy's Eastern Naval Command) to argue that piracy should be treated as terrorism on the sea.

Graph 3 indicates the incidences of deadly violence against passengers/ crew. These are the most affected figures in case of a terrorist strike.

The number of crew killed fell down to 21 as compared to 72 in the year 2000. However, it should be noted that of the 72 casualties in 2000, 57 deaths were due to attacks by terrorists rather than pirates, namely 17 sailors died on USS Cole and 40 deaths were due to a bomb explosion aboard a ferry in Philippines. Thus, the deaths due to piracy in 2000 amounted to 15. The IMB counts terrorist strikes amongst piracy figures as it comes under the gamut of its simplistic definition of piracy. Hence, it shouldn't be inferred looking at the graph that fatal violence is on the decline in piracy attacks. It should be noted that in 1998, at least 22 of the fatalities were attributed to fishermen operating in the Philippines, while the murdered crew of the vessel *Cheung Son*, hijacked in the South China sea, accounted for 23 deaths. In 1997, 33 out of 51 fatalities were crew and shore personnel killed by armed Tamil rebels off Sri Lanka. In applying the techniques of heuristic pattern analysis however, we have to factor in disproportionate impact of single events on such data. The inordinate impact of terrorist strikes in the year 2000 figures is therefore self evident.

Incidents of crew being assaulted have increased. The figures showed an increased use of violence during attacks, particularly the rising number of instances where firearms were used instead of knives. The number of attacks using guns rose from 51 to 73 and the number using knives fell from 132 to 105. These figures must be examined in the light of the overall reduction in the number of attacks in

2001. Thus, the potential for increased violence continues to be a worrying factor.

Although the number of crew killed in 2002 was down to 10 compared to 21 in 2001, that figure concealed a chilling statistic—24 passengers or crew were missing, and most of these must be considered dead. The report's summary of attacks on ships frequently noted that pirates threw crew members into the sea, leaving them to drown.

Hijacking

Post the mid-nineties the figures have nearly been the double which is a worrying factor. Hijacking/missing/detention of 20 odd vessels every year is a deplorable figure. These show the presence of highly organised crime networks capable of handling and misusing ships.

The annual report of the International Chamber of Commerce on piracy showed that while attacks on ships were down by 27% to 335 worldwide in 2001, the number of cases involving the capture and taking of the whole ship doubled from 8 to 16.

ICC said that the increase in hijacking was due to greater involvement in piracy by organized crime networks. These cases normally involve organized crime syndicates. Some of the major cases include *MV Inabukwa, MT Selayang* and *TB Mayang Sari*. The IMB played a key role in the recovery of these three ships.

In 2002, There was a substantial rise in hijacking, up from 16 to 25 incidents. Many involved smaller boats, such as tugs, barges and fishing boats, in the Malacca Straits and Indonesian waters. Crime syndicates in the area were believed to be targeting vessels carrying valuable palm oil and gas oil. For instance one assault involved the tug *Sandia II* off the Sumatran coast and its barge carrying over 3,700 metric tones of palm oil. Local marine police said pirates armed with a gun and knives boarded the tug on 6 September and threw the 18 crew members overboard. Investigators found that the oil-laden barge had later been towed off and renamed to avoid detection.

IMB Director Pottengal Mukundan commented: "In some parts of the world, it is all too easy to board a merchant vessel unlawfully. Against the current concern in respect of maritime terrorism, it is vital that coastal states allocate resources to patrolling their waters more effectively. Failing this, we do not foresee a reduction in these incidents."

Boarding Ships

An analysis of attempted boarding to actual boarding clearly indicates the upward trend in the total number of attempts and actual boarding made by pirates.

The ratios of Boarding to Attempted Boarding have been:

> 1998 – 5.8:1
>
> 1999 – 4.9:1
>
> 2000 – 2.1:1
>
> 2001 – 2.6:1

Although increasing establishment of anti-piracy watches, due vigilance by the crew in affected waters and better awareness have seen decline in this ratio, it is still in alarming proportions. A decreasing success ratio trend in boarding cannot detract from the fact that total number of annual piracy incidences are still increasing.

It is noteworthy that 61% of all categories of attack took place while the victim ship was berthing or at anchor; 39% whilst underway, with the vast majority of these attacks occured in *territorial waters*, which is significant in terms of jurisdiction.

The IMB reported in 2003 that pirate attacks on ships had tripled in the last decade, with a reported 103 attacks in the first three months of the year.

In it's quarterly report, the IMB found the number of attacks in the first three months of the year had already equaled the total number of recorded pirate attacks for the whole of 1993.

The report revealed that Indonesian waters continue to be the world's most dangerous, with 28 pirate attacks recorded between January and March.

Nigeria also recorded a jump in recorded attacks. Nine ships were attacked off Nigerian waters in the first quarter of this year, compared to 6 in 2002.

A total of 145 seafarers were reported killed, assaulted, kidnapped or missing in the first quarter of 2003, with bulk carriers nominated as the vessels most likely to face attack.

Piracy-Terrorism Interface

To summarize, the phenomena of Piracy resurfaced in the last two decades of the previous century. There is a phenomenological and geographical overlap between the phenomena of piracy and terrorism. In most of the regions where piracy is resurfacing, we have large and volatile Muslim populations where Jehadi/fanatical elements/ organisations have been making disturbing in roads. In fact, a number of authorities have called for the equation of piracy with terrorism as it involves violence to the ships crew and passengers. Osama Bin Laden, the Head of the Al Qaida reportedly owns a fleet of 20 ships which he uses for his nefarious purpose of spreading terror and chaos.

Regional Incidence of Piracy-South & South East Asia
Year 2003

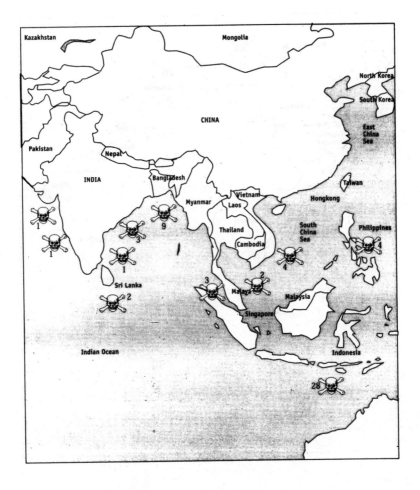

(Source: Data from IMB Piracy Reporting Centre, Kuala Lumpur)

Regional Incidence of Piracy-South America
Year 2003

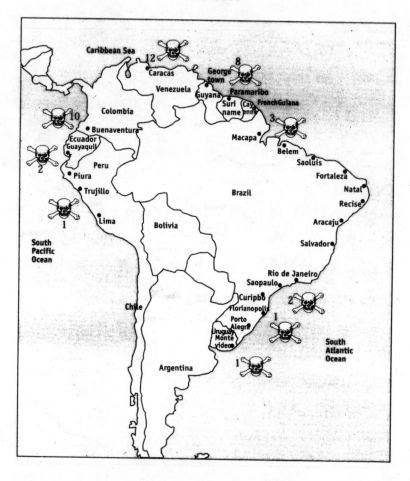

(Source: Data from IMB Piracy Reporting Centre, Kuala Lumpur)

Regional Incidence of Piracy-Africa (2003)
Year 2003

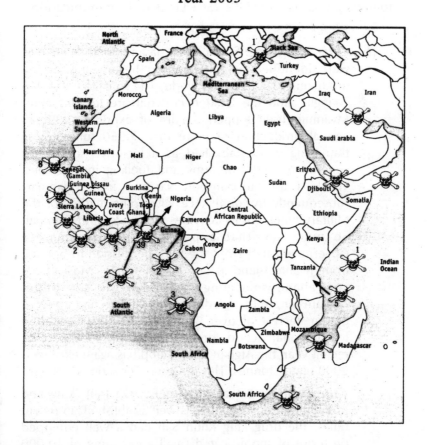

(Source: Data from IMB Piracy Reporting Centre, Kuala Lumpur)

Organised Crime Networks

At the onset of the Millennium, Commander Vijay Sakhuja, a New Delhi based Maritime Analyst, identified the following threats to SLOCs (Sea Lines of Communications)

(a) *Piracy*

(b) *Drug Trafficking*: South East Asia and South West Asia were identified as the two top heroin and opium producing regions of the world. The so called "Golden Triangle" and the Golden crescent are located here. Myanmar itself topped the list of exporters with an annual production of more than 2,360 tones. Drug trafficking was established as a lucrative source for generating funds for arms and fuelling insurgencies. The LTTE used to transport Narcotics from Myanmar; subsequently in connivance with some leaders of the Military Junta, got its activities legitimized in Myanmar. So much so, that apparently the Myanmarese Government had given the LTTE permission to operate from Twante Island at one point of time. Most of the contraband smuggling is through the sea route. Afghanistan, in the heyday of the Taliban, had a record opium harvest of over 3000 metric tons. Concerted international action forced this down. However, in recent year, the Afghan opium crop has again exceeded 2000 metric tonnes. This is a cause for serious concern.

(c) *Gun Running*: Linkage between Drug trafficking and proliferation of small arms is well established. In recent times, the drug king Khun Sah had a well equipped (in terms of sophisticated small arms) army of 10,000 troops to guard his opium cultivation territory in Myanmar. Small boats and fishing trawlers are used to transfer arms to Sri Lanka and Cox Bazaar in Bangladesh. For instance in 1996, Bangladeshi authorities seized 600 rifles aboard a fishing trawler originating in Thailand. Gun running by ships is the safest method. Drug lords have also taken advantage of Singapore's liberal banking laws and money handling opportunities – converting the proceeds of drug sales to gold and smuggling it via Thailand to Myanmar, disturbing the currency situation in the region.

(d) ***Illegal Fishing***: Traditional fishing grounds have been exhausted and competition for newer stocks has been intensified. Fishermen have started encroaching the EEZs (Exclusive Economic Zones) of neighbouring states. For example Thai fishermen regularly plunder fish in the EEZs of Myanmar, India, Malaysia and Indonesia, despite the fact that Thailand is the largest exporter of fish. In 1995, Thai warships clashed with Vietnamese patrol craft attempting to arrest Thai fishing boats, killing two Vietnamese soldiers. In January 1999, a Royal Thai patrol boat, *Tor 99* was fired upon by a Myanmars Naval vessel and returned the fire, as she responded to a distress call by a Thai fishing vessel off the Ramong coast in the Andaman Sea. Such incidents have soured relations between neighbouring littoral states, creating a tense environment. Even the Indian Government has apprehended fishing vessels originating from Pakistan, China, and maritime littorals in the Bay of Bengal.

(e) ***Maritime Pollution***: Major incidents resulting in oil spills have taken place once too often. A large scale spill and subsequent pollution would have devastating economic or environmental disasters. Regional states housing busy shipping lanes have expressed concerns regarding the consequences of a deliberate attack or spill. In Sept 1992, the *MV Ocean Blessing*, a 'rogue' container vessel collided with super tanker *MV Nagasaki Spirit* resulting in a major spillage and fire, killing all 20 crew members on board. A major oil spill could seriously disrupt or close down a strategic SLOC like the Malacca Strait, choking oil supplies to various states in Asia Pacific.

(f) ***Human Smuggling***: The International Labour Organisation said that more than 50% of Asians abroad were illegal immigrants. One estimate said that on an average one million people are smuggled the world over every year and smuggling by sea is the cheapest and easiest form of illegal transportation of migrants. In 1999 itself, 100 Chinese stowaways were found in ships sailing for California, Vancouver and British Colombia.

(g) ***Mines:*** A major threat, sea mines are the cheapest form of maritime warfare. Commodore Jeo, Chief of Singapore Navy, has said that sea mines can be used to disrupt freedom of navigation in the Malacca Strait. An example which defines the threat is the damage caused to 18 Merchant vessels in the Red Sea in July 1984 due to mines laid by Libyan interests, solely to show 'indignation against Egypt'.

The whole maritime infrastructure has several loopholes which can be exploited. The system is prone to fraud, hijack, smuggling and other crimes time and time again. Lack of effective legal control and resources, and certain shortcomings of the industry such as Flags Of Convenience shipping have bred crime syndicates which thrive on these soft spots. An overview of IMB's recent reports highlights these fairly innocuous and underrated illegal activities which have a huge potential for exploitation by terrorists.

Hijackings, Kidnappings and Ransom

As mentioned earlier the number of hijackings have witnessed a major and steady increase since the year 2000. These imply increased involvement by organised crime networks. Pottengal Mukundan, Director of ICC's Commercial Crime Services, said, "The hijacking of a whole ship and the resale of its cargo requires huge resources and detailed planning. It typically involves a mother ship from which to launch the attack, a supply of automatic weapons, false identity papers for the crew and vessel, fake cargo documents, and a broker network to sell the stolen goods illegally."[1]

There have been cases reported where tugs towing barges carrying expensive cargoes have been hijacked, and the cargo is either transferred to a pirate vessel or is taken along with the barge, the barges name changed to avoid identification. According to IMB Director Pottengal Mukundan, these case highlights the risks of moving goods by tug, and the need for extra care.

During 2001, a new trend in piracy emerged in the Northern part of the Malacca Straits in the waters off Aceh. Pirates attacked and kidnapped crewmembers demanding ransom for their safe returns. This "kidnap and ransom" trend previously was confined to Somali waters. Within two months there were two similar incidents off Aceh involving *MT Tirta Niaga IV* and *TB Ocean Silver*. The amount demanded by these pirates is normally not exorbitant and ship owners pay to avoid complications. The IMB believes that there may be more such incidents, which may have gone unreported because owners are being threatened and warned not to report to the Authorities. The Indonesian Authorities were notified and are said to have intensified patrols in the area. The Free Aceh Movement, which had threatened to disrupt shipping in the Straits of Malacca was blamed for the incidents by the Indonesian Authorities.[2]

Phantom Ship Fraud

In September 2002, the owner of a missing cargo of palm oil worth US$ 2.5 million was defeated in his court battle to recover insurance for the loss. The ship carrying the cargo disappeared on the high seas along with its captain and crew. The *Pacifica* left from a Malaysian port in 1998, but never reached her official destination, Beihai in China. Investigations later revealed that neither the chartering nor ship owners' companies had ever existed, and that their official Manila address was false. The identity papers of captain and crew were also shown to be forged. At the trial, the ICC's International Maritime Bureau (IMB) said the case showed all the signs of a Phantom Ship fraud, and gave expert evidence on what constitutes a Phantom Ship Operation—when a vessel chartered by criminals is loaded with goods, and then given a complete identity change after leaving port. Instead of sailing to the contractual destination, Phantom Ship Operators steal the cargo and discharge it illegally at a different port using fake identity papers for the vessel and cargo.[3]

In 2003, the IMB found in an investigation that multi-million dollar cargoes are at risk of being stolen by an organised criminal group based in Lebanon. The IMB reported that a cell is operating at least two vessels off the Eastern Mediterranean, North Africa, and West African coasts, duping their victims out of cargoes. This gang is connected to at least three cases of deviation and appropriation of cargoes. By offering bargain freight rates to shippers operating on the Eastern Mediterranean and North African coasts, the vessels' operators are easily obtaining cargo. Rather than discharging the cargo at the originally contracted port, the vessels have been changing identity and illegally discharging the cargoes at other ports. The cargo is often sold at reduced rates to another buyer. The cargo owner's suspicions regarding delay in delivery of goods are invariably allayed 'by excuses ranging from bad weather to technical difficulties. "The cargoes being targeted are those that are easily disposed off. The chances of recovering any cargo stolen this way are minimal," said IMB Director Captain Pottengal Mukundan.[4]

The first reported case of such cargo theft in this region was in September 2002 when a Honduran-registered, Marshall Islands-owned ship loaded steel cargo in Istanbul and headed for Lagos, Nigeria. The 30 year old general cargo vessel deviated from its charted route, and wound up illegally selling the cargo in Lattakia, Syria. In November 2002, the same vessel, having changed her name and now flying under the Tongan flag, was chartered to take a consignment of polyethylene from Libya to Morocco. Once again, she headed to Lattakia and quickly discharged the cargo under false documentation. The IMB has learned that since leaving Lattakia, the ship had again changed names.[5]

In the most recent case, in December 2002, a totally different general-cargo carrier built in 1980, purportedly flying the North Korean flag, loaded a shipment of bagged cement in Alexandria, Egypt. The shipment was intended for two consignees in Conakry, Guinea. Again, the ship's identity was changed at sea. This time the cargo was redirected to Banjul, Gambia, where the cement was peddled to a local buyer. Fortunately, the vessel was apprehended after a chance contact with an alert local agent in Banjul. The case is currently under investigation by local authorities. The three recent cases have sparked renewed concern about a possible resurgence of ship deviations from ports in this region. This was a widespread problem in the 1980s, but has subsided for some years.[6]

Flags of Convenience

The thriving fleets of FOC (Flags Of Convenience) [7] vessels is a major legal loophole that terrorists can well exploit with ease. An FOC ship is a vessel that flies the flag of a country other than the country of ownership. It enables owners to avoid high registration fees and taxes, and to employ cheap labour under sub-standard conditions, its easier to evade audits and compromise assessments. In some cases, private companies rather than the administration may run the national ship registry. For example, Liberia's registry is run by a US private company.[8] Some countries' regulations are shockingly loose. In the case of Cambodia, ship owners can even register their vessels online, meaning there is an absolute minimum of regulation. It ensures that vetting of cargos and crews is kept to a minimum. Shipping sources say that most boat owners often have little idea who is manning their vessels. On many badly-run boats, crews are brought in from developing countries and paid low wages and housed in poor conditions. It becomes all the more easier to facilitate infiltration by criminals. [9]Among the 30 FOC registries, Bahamas, Liberia and Panama are known to possess large merchant fleets accounting for about half the total percentage of global merchant shipping tonnage. [10] There is widespread practice of 'flag hopping' wherein on the slightest indication of crackdown by authorities, the identified vessel quickly changes its flag, papers and name, making it harder to be traced. FOC has resulted in crime syndicates and terror cells using it to avoid detection and indulge in drug / weapons / human trafficking and fraudulent shipping.

Questionable Background of Crew

This is currently the most serious source of threat to maritime shipping. Crewmembers of merchant vessels belong to different nationalities.

According to the International Maritime Bureau (IMB), it is virtually impossible to verify the authenticity of the identity of the crew. Clearly, the ships' crew themselves can act as a potential threat. Both the Philippines and Indonesia are the largest suppliers of merchant ship crews. These states are home to radical groups like the Abu Sayaf Group (ASG) and Free Aceh Movement rebels. Under the circumstances, it is virtually impossible to detect potentially undesirable crew members. The situation gets more complicated in case of vessels that fly 'flags of convenience' that employ multinational crews. It is virtually impossible to verify the authenticity of the identity of the crew. A significant problem in this context is that of counterfeit and improperly issued mariner documentation, particularly among the third world seafarer supplying countries. The IMB has issued a warning to ship operators about the thousands of unqualified crew and masters working illegally with false papers and has called for tighter security by authorities issuing certificates. The alert follows the release of statistics showing that of 54 maritime administrations surveyed, more than 12,000 cases of forged certificates of competency were reported.[11] The IMB also believes that, at times, the issuing authorities themselves are to blame. For instance, the Coast Guard office in Puerto Rico was reported to have issued approximately 500 suspicious certificates of competency.[12] Such cases usually escape detection by the port authorities. Fake papers for boats and crew members can also be bought and sold easily. Several investigations by industry bodies have proved that licenses for even senior crew members can be quickly obtained with no security vetting. David Cockcroft, General Secretary of the International Transport Workers Federation said that he bought a senior mate's license from Panama for just $4,000 and two passport photos. 'I am not qualified for that, but it was easy,' he stated.[13]

For vessels which do not fall under the gamut of such a nexus or are operated by incompetent crew, there is no guarantee that it is not being used for some nefarious business without the knowledge of the crew. A lapse in standard anti-stowaway checks and controlled access, may lead to the vessel being used as a vector for transporting illegal and dangerous substances, or human stowaways. There are sufficient spaces internal to the vessel, (especially large ones) which can be employed for the purpose. There have been cases of underwater welding done by smugglers on the stern of vessels to transport drugs. Thus, a vigilant watch by the crew involved is an absolute necessity.

Twin Shadow of Terrorism

Thus, as can be inferred from the trends in maritime crime—the set up is prone to be exploited by organized crime syndicates who have shown resourcefulness, daring and tactical ingenuity to dupe shipping interests as well as prey on vessels transiting affected waters. With the evolution in their structuring and a more developed responsiveness to any sort of curbing oriented legal initiatives, their threat has increased manifold. What is worse still, is the possible 'sell over' or duplication of these networks by terrorist cells interested in exploiting these for hiding assets, illegal arms/human transfer and – for terrorist attacks on warships, cruise liners, large ships with valuable cargoes, ports and busy shipping lanes.

There is a need to investigate this crime-terror nexus. All the above mentioned activities and tactics are no more a part of speculation. Terrorists have been detected time and again indulging in these operations. There is an urgent need to identify these cells and disrupt their functioning before the crime-terror nexus grows into a major threat.

In its meeting held in February 2002, the Council for Security Co-operation in the Asia-Pacific (CSCAP) Working Group on Maritime Co-operation examined the contents of the phenomena "maritime terrorism". The working group used a relatively broad definition of maritime terrorism.[14] According to the group, maritime terrorism refers to the undertaking of terrorist acts and activities:-

(1) Within the marine environment,

(2) Using or against vessels or fixed platforms at sea or in port, or against any one of their passengers or personnel.

(3) Against coastal facilities or settlements, including tourist resorts, port areas, and port town or cities.

Voluntarily vague, the definition adopted did not define either terrorist acts and activities or what is included under marine environment. Criminal acts and activities undertaken for a political purpose can be qualified as terrorism. Hence, maritime terrorism was implied to be distinct from piracy, which was viewed to be committed for purely personal gains. The use of the expression marine environment is wise, since it does not distinguish between the international law classification of high seas and territorial waters (criminal attacks against ships tend to happen, generally, in territorial waters.)[15]

The IMB has been for some time, calling for piracy to be given the status of maritime terrorism. Is marine terrorism so distinct from piracy, as is generally assumed, and vehemently contradicted by the IMB? A brief look at the geography and reports of possible setups of marine terrorist networks will help define the issue even better.

Though on the surface, there have been no discernable geographical areas for maritime targets, and terrorist have struck in Latin America, Europe, Middle East, Asia-Pacific and in South and South East Asia. However, among the two dozen terrorist groups identified to have been engaged in maritime terrorism, approximately nine are currently active and five of these operate in the Asia Pacific region.[16] The geography of the Asia Pacific region indicates that terrorist hubs in Asia are located in the littorals: LTTE in Jaffna, Sri Lanka; Al Qaida in Yemen, Somalia, Singapore and Pakistan; the Abu·Sayyaf Group in the Philippines, the Free Aceh Movement in Indonesia. Thus, the Asia Pacific region is currently the focus of terrorism at sea. This is augmented with the Golden Crescent – Golden Triangle, high sea piracy region. Moreover, these groups have built sophisticated organisations that run an efficient network of commercial as also terrorist activities, pursuing their business with total impunity, much of the industrial infrastructure and wealth are concentrated in these littorals (coastal regions), which also serve as nodes for transport of trade and culture, as also the hub of illegal activity, be it contraband trade, drug smuggling, gun running or human smuggling. Future conflicts are expected to take place in the littorals, i.e. where the sea meets the land. These also house a large proportion of world population.[17]

A worldwide investigation of terrorist financing which included merchant shipping and flag-of-convenience vessel registries was initiated in 2001. The, probe was to center on 80 front companies controlled in 50 countries by wealthy Saudi Arabian exile and terrorist mastermind Osama Bin Laden and his Al Qaida network of radical Islamic fundamentalists. The Bin Laden holdings were later found to include "shipping concerns". In a dispatch reporting the initiation of this probe by David Osler in the London-based Lloyd's list published on Sept. 28, 2001, potential operational benefits for terrorists in owning ships were seen as obvious and considerable. Osler wrote. "Access to merchant vessels would give them sure-fire ways to smuggle personnel and equipment—and perhaps even biological or nuclear weapons—into any littoral state in the world."

"Trawling registers for such details of shipping company ownership that are available to the public is possible," but he added: "Under the flag of convenience system, Bin Laden vessels could be registered anywhere in the world, including countries that would not attract suspicion. How ever such is the secrecy maintained by many flags of convenience that establishing ownership may often prove extremely hard." One investigator quoted by Osler likened the records verification to the proverbial hunt for "a needle in a haystack." Osler quoted "one prominent mercenary specializing in armed ship recoveries" as saying: "I would be amazed if Al Qaida were not ship owners. Ships represent major investment. You can hide several millions with a tanker."

A shipbroker in Germany admitted to acting as a translator when Washed al Hagen – (sought in connection with the 1998 bombings of two US embassies in East Africa) – an Al Qaida operative, attempted to buy a merchant vessel.[18] Bin Laden and the Al Qaida terror network are now known to own or have chartered approximately 20 merchant vessels suspected to possess 'flag of convenience' (FOC) registry in Liberia, Panama and the Isles of Man, and capable of undertaking ocean passage.

There have been occasions where such shipments have been detected and captured. Terrorists have been intercepted on container vessels ensconced in containers. As usual chinks in the armour were fully exploited. In another example, on January 3, 2002 the Israeli navy captured *Karine-A*, a Palestinian Authority ship, carrying 50 tons of lethal ammunition, making full use of a change in nomenclature to evade detection. The ship was sailing in international waters on its way to the Suez Canal. The shipment reportedly included both 122 mm and 107 mm Katyusha rockets, which have ranges of 20 and 8 kilometers respectively. It also contained 80 mm and 120 mm mortar shells, various types of anti-tank missiles, anti-tank mines, sniper rifles, Kalashnikov rifles and ammunition. From Gaza, the 122 mm Katyushas could have threatened Ashkelon and other coastal cities; while from the West Bank, Ben-Gurion International Airport and several major Israeli cities would have been within their range. The shipment also included rubber boats and diving equipment, which would have facilitated sea borne attacks from Gaza against coastal cities. According to the Lloyds, the vessel was owned by the Beirut-based Diana K Shipping Company and registered in Lebanon. Its original name was Rim K and was purchased by Ali Mohammed Abbas, an Iraqi national for $400,000 in August 2001 and was re-registered in Tonga as the *Karine – A*.

As noted earlier, one of Bin Laden's cargo freighters unloaded supplies in Kenya for the suicide cadres who subsequently bombed the US embassies in Kenya and Tanzania.

The LTTE (Liberation Tigers of Tamil Elam) of Sri Lanka owns and charters ships which are engaged in the movements of narcotics from Myanmar to Turkey. From there the contraband goes onto ports in USA and Europe. The LTTE has a fleet of 10-12 well maintained Freighters flying Panamian, Honduran or Liberian flag. The majority of Cargo they carry is legitimate (hard board, coconut, fertilizers etc). However, about 5 percent capacity is utilised to smuggle weapons, ammunition, explosives and Narcotics.

Thus, in an era of globalization, it is easy for terrorists to indulge in narcotics/ human smuggling, gun /contraband trade etc., bulk of which is carried over the sea. Unfortunately, maritime shipping, in particular FOC registry, is the soft under-belly of the maritime world. It offers the best vehicle to transport terrorist-owned weapons and a safe haven for terrorist-sponsored subversive activity at sea.[19] And if the crime networks dealing with similar activities are allowed to develop further, terrorists won't have to try much harder establishing some of their own. A crackdown on such networks will prevent a possible future adoption by the terrorists of the existing means. Hence action against terrorism ought to incorporate destruction of these crime syndicates as well.

Terror Attacks On Sea

Terrorist strikes on the high seas are no longer the staple of fiction or hypothesis. There has been a large number of significant incidents and strikes which should make us sit up and take note.

Other than using shipping as a means, there have been several incidents of terrorist strikes on the shipping industry itself. A few of the major ones are mentioned here, to define the reality of the impact and threat presented so far to shipping.

The LTTE is one of the most ruthless and dangerous terrorist groups in the world. It is active in sea piracy, smuggling, gun running, narcotics, money laundering, abduction and assassinations. The LTTE has engaged in wolf pack tactics, used high-speed boats filled with explosives and rammed into naval vessels. It is reported to be experimenting with a human suicide torpedo.[20]

In 1961, political insurgents had embarked the Portuguese passenger liner *Santa Maria*. They took over the ship as a revolt against Salazar and Franco in the African colonies and on the Iberian peninsula. Their plan was to sail the vessel to Fernando Po, subsequently seize Spanish Guinea and finally launch an attack on Angola.

On July 11, 1988, *City of Poros*, a Greek cruise ferry carrying 500 tourists was attacked by terrorists. Three terrorists belonging to the Abu Nidal Organisation (ANO) boarded the vessel, opened fire with submachine guns and tossed hand grenades onto the deck killing at least nine persons and injuring approximately 100 others. The ANO had planned to hold the passengers hostage against the release of Palestinian prisoners in Israel.

Hijacking of the Italian cruise vessel *Achille Lauro* in October 1985 emerged as the turning point in the history of modem maritime terrorism. Four heavily armed Palestine Liberation Front (PLF) terrorists hijacked the *Achille Lauro*, carrying more than 400 passengers and crew, off Egypt. The hijackers demanded that Israel free 50 Palestinian prisoners. The terrorists killed a disabled American tourist and threw his body overboard. After a two-day drama, the hijackers surrendered in exchange for a pledge of safe passage. This incident sparked off a series of security measures being adopted on passenger ships all around the globe. But the industry never really recovered to full potential. Post 9/11, the Hotel and Tourism Industry experienced a major decline in business. Fewer passengers have been embarking on liners. Renaissance Cruise, a major corporation in this sector, filed for bankruptcy, stating that it was a victim of the fallout of terrorism.[21] Similarly, the London-based P&O Princess Cruises and the US-based Royal Caribbean announced a merger noting that ships around the world were half-empty.[22] These events highlight the brittle nature of the cruise industry when exposed to terrorist threats. It has the potential to undermine the root business interests of the industry. It would be interesting to note that pirates plundering a cruise vessel would have equivalent effects and far reaching consequences.

On October 12, 2000, *USS Cole*, an Arleigh Burke-class destroyer was attacked by terrorists in Aden harbour, Yemen. While the ship was refueling offshore, a small craft, filled with explosives, approached the ship and exploded. It was a major security lapse on the part of the ship's duty staff to allow any unidentified vessel to pull up along side of the Cole. In both the cases of *USS Cole* and the *Limburg*, the French supertanker attacked in October 2002 in Yemen territorial waters, a small boat packed with explosives (which tore open the hulls of the vessels) was involved.

A report by Lloyd's Register shipping service on the *Limburg* case explained that the location of the hole at the waterline, with its jagged metal edge facing inwards and the absence of any noticeable blast damage to the deck of the vessel support the theory of deliberate attack. It is noteworthy that in 1993, almost all the weapons and explosives used to create bomb blasts and mayhem in the major Indian port city and metropolis of Mumbai were brought by sea, with the boats offloading their consignments in several small ports dotting the West Coast of India. The Abu Sayaaf group in the Philippines staged the Bali bombings in 2002, to advertise the survival of the Al Qaida cells in the post 9/11 era.

Mumbai Bomb Blast and Bali

There have been a number of terrorist attacks and arson cases, the ones which had the maximum strategic impact, and provide an idea of the potential targets and consequences on the industry, have been mentioned above. From 1999 to 2003 there have been another spate of bomb attacks in Mumbai. These are being covered in more detail subsequently in the book. The most recent such attack occured in Spain in Madrid in Mar 2004. It left 200 people dead and some 1500 wounded

Let us come back to the IMB's call for piracy to be termed as maritime terrorism. What would be the strategic implication of such status being allotted to piracy and other maritime crime?

Certain critics had pointed out that terrorist strikes figures were being included in piracy attacks to 'jack up the total figures for piracy..' and press was still somewhat dismissive of piracy reaching any alarming proportions as yet.

However the fact that the trend has been observed to be simply increasing cannot be totally ignored, in 2003 itself, without any incidence of terrorist strikes the nature of reports (involving arms and violence) and other figures have increased.

If terrorists indulge in piracy, hijacking and illegal smuggling, so do the crime lords as these are based on the shortcomings inherent in the system. Political gain or personal, the modus operandi are the same.

New Face of Piracy
Piracy today increasingly involves:-

- Usage of arms and sophisticated weaponry such as hull penetration capable rocket launchers

- Millions of dollars are at stake whenever a vessel, its crew or cargo falls in the unscrupulous hands of a criminal and major trade can be affected.

- It has merited intervention of forces employing warships, and that many a time international cooperation between various navies was resorted to tackle it.

Terrorist groups like the LTTE have begun to increasingly exploit the existing piracy network. Today, each act of piracy could be a potential terrorist move. Hence, piracy being accorded the adage of terrorism will practically combat terrorism in at least some indirect ways. This would result in more comprehensive action on the part of States with shipping interests. Present initiatives are not enough as the trend of piracy incidents is still increasing.

Any analysis of crime patterns at sea is automatically an analysis of terrorist capabilities. This fact assumes more importance on sea than in any other medium. Any suppressive action against crime networks is action against a potential terrorist network too. For it is not a question of definition; but its impact. If upgrading the status of piracy to terrorism serves to best diminish the possibility of a terrorist strike or exploitation, (which appears to be the case) then the status should be given with immediate effect, especially whilst formulating any policy for terror strike deterrence.

International Action

The industry is waking up to the challenges posed by organised crime and terrorism. The legal, economic and political implications of threats to maritime security materialising is now recognised by most states and players in the sector.

ICC International Maritime Bureau (IMB)[23]

The first ICC anti-crime bureau, the International Maritime Bureau, was founded in 1981, chiefly to counter maritime fraud as a division of the International Chamber of Commerce Crime Services Arm. It quickly received the support of the International Maritime Organization in a resolution urging governments and law enforcement agencies to co-operate with the new body. More recently, it was granted observer status with Interpol. The International Shipping Federation, a major trade association of owners-operators worked together with the IMO in the 1980s to provide impetus for actions against piracy.

It is essentially a Maritime Trade Association, operating on the international level and represents the interests of the shipping industry. IMB's task is to prevent fraud in international trade and maritime transport, reduce the risk of piracy and assist law enforcement in protecting crews. It tracks cargos and shipments and verifies their arrival at scheduled ports.

Much of IMB's work concerns prevention in the form of timely advice on how to reduce corporate vulnerability to fraud and malpractice. In the event of frauds and piratical attacks it carries out investigations with a view to bringing perpetrators to justice and recovering losses. Other specific tasks are to:

- Authenticate suspect bills of lading and other documents.
- Disseminate information on maritime crime that has been collected from commercial, government and international sources.
- Offer due diligence advice.
- Propose ways for victims of fraudulent transactions to extricate themselves and minimize the damage.

- Provide legal advice and support in litigation.
- Raise awareness of the dangers of maritime crime and provide training in counter-measures.

Today, Governments of the world's leading trading nations support the bureau's work. IMB's multidisciplinary staff and contacts worldwide gather information and respond swiftly in cases of maritime fraud or when ships are attacked on the high seas. IMB today covers all types of fraud and malpractice in trading and transport.

A fortnightly confidential bulletin lists frauds, commercial failures and non-payment of debts. This is supplemented by a credit report service on companies engaged in shipping and trading. Additionally, the bureau runs a ship monitoring and supercargo service. Another programme checks the credentials of ship owners and prospective charterers before a vessel is fixed.

The IMB Piracy Reporting Center[24]

Outrage in the shipping industry at the alarming growth in piracy on the world's oceans prompted the creation of the IMB Piracy Reporting Center in October 1992 in Kuala Lampur. The Center is financed by voluntary contributions from a number of companies[25] and provides its services free of charge to all vessels irrespective of ownership or flag.

Services

- To receive reports of suspicious or unexplained craft movements, boarding and armed robbery from ships and to alert other ships and law enforcement agencies in the area.
- To issue status reports of piracy and armed robbery via daily broadcasts on Inmarsat-C through its Safety NET service. Ships can also obtain these status reports by contacting the Center.

- To collate and analyze information received and issue consolidated reports to relevant bodies, including the International Maritime Organization.

- To assist owners and crews of ships that have been attacked.

- To locate vessels that have been seized by pirates and recover stolen cargoes.

Piracy Reporting Service

The IMB Piracy Reporting Center maintains a round-the-clock watch every day of the year. In close collaboration with law enforcement, the Center acts on reports of suspicious shipping movements, piracy and armed robbery at sea anywhere in the world. The Center broadcasts daily status bulletins to ships at sea. These broadcasts cover Africa, Middle East, Indian Sub continent, South East Asia, the Far East, Central America, South America and the Caribbean Waters. Quarterly reports are made available to interested bodies, including the International Maritime Organization. Weekly piracy report are posted on the Internet with weekly updates of attacks and warnings. The report is compiled from the piracy reporting service's daily status bulletins. The regular reports contain details of the location and nature of attacks and allow companies to put their ship masters on special alert when they are passing through waters in which recent piratical attacks have been reported. IMB compiles Quarterly, Annual and Special Reports and publishes the center's Annual Report, "Piracy and Armed Robbery Against Ships."

The PRC is clubbing together the data on acts of piracy and terrorism as both are covered under the fabric of its simplistic functional definition. It is essential that from the legal standpoint, piracy be equated with terrorism. Their common aim is exploitation and subsequent destabilization of governments and civilized societies. Piracy and such violent incidents must therefore be seen as tributaries of maritime terrorism and must be dealt with as such.

Maritime Co-operation and Arrangements

After the September 11 terror attacks in the US, much concern has been directed towards the security of ports and ships. Piracy is also endemic and on the rise. That raises the real possibility that Al-Qaida cells would not have to infiltrate a crew, but could simply hijack the boat, take it over and steer it to their target. *It would be a grim water-borne mirror image of the hijacked planes crashing into New York and the Pentagon.* It is not impossible for hijackers or terrorist to hijack ships particularly LNG, LPG or large tankers to undergo suicide missions for their cause. Forged ship documents and crew travel documents can easily be obtained with the right connections. IMB Director Pottengal Mukundan commented: "In some parts of the world it is all too easy to board a merchant vessel unlawfully. Against the current concern in respect of maritime terrorism, it is vital that coastal states allocate resources to patrolling their waters more effectively. Failing this, we do not foresee a reduction in these incidents."

The IMB annual piracy report for 2002 said that attacks like the one in the Gulf of Aden in October, when the French tanker Limburg was rammed by a boat packed with explosives, were difficult to prevent. "No shipboard response can protect the ship in these circumstances."

The only answer was for coastal states to make sure that approaches to their ports were secure. IMB recommended that port authorities designate approach channels under coast guard or police supervision from which all unauthorized craft would be banned.

"The risk of terrorist attack can perhaps never be eliminated, but sensible steps can be taken to reduce the risk," the IMB said. "The issue here is how seriously do the governments take the threat of maritime terrorism...Post-Limburg, we cannot continue to hope for the best and ignore the lessons." The SUA Convention (Suppression of Unlawful Acts Against Safety of Maritime Navigation Convention) allows sovereign governments to prosecute criminals operating in their territorial waters.

Although governments take considerable actions to prevent terrorism in their territorial waters and are also proactive on the high seas, they are unable to protect national merchant fleets in territorial waters of another sovereign states. Under these circumstances, the only effective response to global terrorism is inter-governmental co-operation. Given the limitations of any nation to handle or unilaterally respond to multiple threats, co-operation among states is extremely important.

The very fact that as many as 10 navies from Asia, Europe and the Persian Gulf were deployed to either carry out strikes in Afghanistan, or intercept vessels suspected of carrying terrorists, is a pointer towards the growing relevance and importance of multinational naval co-operation. The US realised it would need the support as it mounted a major operation in Western Arabian Sea (off the coast of Pakistan) to try and intercept Bin Laden and other Al Qaida operatives should they try to escape by sea. As is well known, during the American offensive against the Taliban and Al Qaida in Afghanistan, the Indian Navy sent its ships to escort high value American logistics vessels through the Straits of Malacca. Two Indian Navy Off Shore Patrol Vessels (OPVs) were employed for these escort duties through these vulnerable straits for almost one year. This operation was code named 'Op Sagittarius'.

While considering naval co-operation, maritime security analyst, Rahoul Roy Choudhry has outlined that naval co-operation whether bilateral or multilateral comprises a wide variety of activities differing in scale, complexity and sensitivity and that at the 'higher level' would involve, activities such as information and Intelligence exchanges, joint and multilateral exercises, warship design, maintenance and construction, avoidance of Incidents at Sea (INSEA) agreements, joint operations in peacetime, co-ordinated patrols (anti-piracy, etc.), co-operative maritime surveillance, enhanced interoperability stressing "joint- ness", joint doctrine development, mine countermeasures, combined SLOC protection, and, finally, the establishment of standing regional naval forces and joint operations in warfare. These activities are also directly linked to the prevailing set of political relationships. In view of the common threats, nation states do need to establish a strategic relationship and it must be borne in mind that the implications of multilateral naval exercises are far greater than those of bilateral exercises.

There is a crying need for co-ordination of the effort at the global level and for timely generation of precise intelligence. *As Vice Admiral Das of the Indian Navy points out, the threat must be countered where it originates and not where it is delivered.*[26] Commander PK Banerjee in a paper presented at the Sixth Asia-Pacific Naval College seminar in Tokyo on 28 Jan 03, highlighted as an example the financial assistance and expertise provided by Japan to Indonesia to set up the Anti-Piracy Center at Batam Island and stressed on the need to choke the 'end destination' of pirated goods (most pirated ships and goods are sold at several known ports of disrepute in North Asia, Africa, South – East Asia and even South Asia.

The IMO is currently carrying out a survey of the legislations of various nations so that the anti-piracy campaign gets more legal teeth. For example in an incident involving the Japanese vessel, *Alondra Rainbow*, the hijackers who had been apprehended by the Indian Coast Guard could not be tried for fourteen months because the Indian Penal Code has no specific provisions to deal with Piracy. Action was ultimately taken under the section of armed robbery. The action was welcomed and applauded by the shipping community. The incident highlighted the importance of special forces to board vessels and apprehend culprits, as also the relevance of close co-operation between the Indian Navy, Coast Guard, the PRC and the Indian government. The 14 convicted pirates will all serve seven years of "rigorous imprisonment"—the Indian version of hard labour.

The Indian convictions also follow a recent Chinese court decision to sentence the hijackers of the tanker *Siam Xanxai* to between 10 and 15 years imprisonment.

In contrast, the Indonesians recently sentenced the hijackers of the *Inabukwa* to between two and four years imprisonment, according to Captain Mukundan.[27]

The Indian court action was undertaken under Article 105 of the United Nations Convention on the Law Of the Sea (UNCLOS).

There is a need to strengthen domestic legislation on the issue and make the international definition more specific and effective.

Legal initiatives around the globe should be uniform and as mentioned, suitably effective.

Institutional Framework

The International Maritime Organisation at its meeting on Maritime Security in London (2003) made the significant recommendation that piracy at sea be treated as maritime terrorism and put on the agenda of the ongoing Global War against terrorism. It would be essential for the U.N. and other international agencies to step in to ensure that actions are taken to actualize this. The U.N. already uses the piracy data provided by the IMB.

The Third United Nations Convention on The Law of the Sea in November 1982 (UNCLOS III), had the following main provisions relevant to maritime and Naval co-operation: articles 98, 100, 108, 192, 194, 276 and 277. Under article 100 pertaining to anti-piracy, states are required to co-operate in the repression of piracy on the high seas. Article 105 goes on to state, "On the high seas or in any other place outside the jurisdiction of any state, every state may seize a pirate ship or aircraft, or a ship or aircraft undertaken by piracy and under the control of the pirates, and arrest the persons and seize the property on board." Article 108, regarding illicit trafficking in drugs requires states to co-operate in the suppression of illicit trafficking in narcotic drugs engaged in by ships on the high seas.

A major shortcoming of the UNCLOS III is that it does not provide any guidelines on the establishment of institutional arrangements required for the implementation of these provisions. The majority of attacks at present occur within territorial waters, they fall outside the UNCLOS legal definition of piracy which defines it as illegal acts of violence or detention committed for private purposes on the high seas.

There is an urgent need to establish institutions, regional arrangements and organizations which deal with these security issues. Example of such an organization is the CSCAP mentioned earlier. It has been doing tremendous work in the field of maritime cooperation. This is essentially a "second track" organization, whose ideas feed directly into the "first track" 21–member ASEAN Regional Forum (ARF) and influence its decisions. The ARF is the only high –level intergovernmental organization which discusses security issues in the Asia-Pacific. India is a full member.[28]

The Maritime Working Group (MWG) of CSCAP, one of the five working groups of the organisation, deals directly with maritime security issues. It has helped improve the security situation in the region, including provision of guidelines, published literature and information on maritime and naval affairs.

It should be noted that at the international level the U.N. plays a pivotal role in ocean affairs, through cooperation with other global and regional institutions.[29] The acceptance and implementation of these Conventions and Programmes by States form the basis of international co-operation in maritime affairs. Two U.N. bodies–the Intergovernmental Oceanographic Commission (ICO) of the United Nations Educational, Scientific and Cultural Organisation (UNESCO) and the IMO are directly involved in maritime affairs[30]. The IMO has added the International Ships and Port facilities Security Code (ISPS Code) as an appendix to its International Convention for the Safety Of Life At Sea, 1974 (SOLAS). This code lays down mandatory security requirements and recommended procedures for ships, shipping companies and international port facilities handling these vessels. This code is dealt with in subsequent chapters.

In December 2001, Singapore authorities arrested 15 suspected Islamic militants, with links to the Al Qaida, planning to blow up US naval vessels and a bus that was to transport American military service personnel.

A tape released by the Singapore government features a man describing how explosives could be carried on a bicycle without arousing suspicion. One plot involved bombing US Navy vessels in a special "kill zone" along the northeastern shores of Singapore and the bus that was targeted carried US military personnel between a naval base used by visiting warships and a train station. The US Navy has a logistics unit in Singapore, and warships going to and from Afghanistan have been docked for replenishment in the new naval facility specially designed to accommodate US aircraft carriers. The Al Qaida therefore is down but not out. Massive bombs blast have taken place recently as under:-

- **Bali**   12 Oct 2002, with 202 people killed
- **Istanbul**   15 and 20 Nov 2003, 63 people killed
- **Casablanca** 16 May 2003. 45 people killed
- **Karbala**   02 Mar 2004. 140 Shias killed
- **Madrid**   11 Mar 2004 (or 3/11) 201 killed in bombings on four trains.

There is a need to develop new responses to challenges from asymmetric threats such as terrorism. The relevant tools could include vulnerability assessments, action plans, quick response teams and damage assessment. A model port guide, with special attention to security guidelines, counter-terrorism, contingency plans, real-time cargo, people, vessel tracking systems and rigorous analytic models, needs to be prepared and implemented in all Indian ports. It is important to harness off-the-shelf technologies. Co-operation helps to deploy powerful forces to bear at the best place, at the right moment, resulting in a rapid and overwhelming response. Post-September 11, international initiatives have indicated that combating terrorism requires commonality of purpose, opinion, interests, values and a co-coordinated approach to combat forces inimical to peace and security. Even a country as powerful as the United States could not have gone ahead unilaterally to counter terrorism. It needed international co-operation to track terrorists, quickly deploy military forces, undertake surveillance, obtain tactical Intelligence, base facilities, or even to over-fly national air spaces. An example of such international co-operation was provided by the hijacking of the Alondra Rainbow, a Japanese merchant vessel by pirates in November 1999. As will be elaborated in greater detail subsequently, the vessel was finally captured.

The September 11 attacks on civil aviation, raised the spectre of similar attacks on passenger ships. At the World Tourism Organisation's 14th General Assembly and the Millennium Conference of Tourism Leaders in October 2001, held at Osaka, Japan, the participants were unanimous in their opinion that '*terrorism is the direct enemy of tourism*. There is little doubt that the tourism industry faces a major crisis situation and it will take some time for it to recover from the fallout of the September 11 attacks.

The Tourism industry is aware of its high profile nature and is conscious of the fact that what happens on one cruise liner affects the entire industry. The events of September 11, 2001, have severely damaged the tourism sector and could threaten up to approximately nine million jobs worldwide. The *Achille Lauro* incident was a wake-up call that resulted in the introduction of several security measures like boarding through metal detectors, hand baggage checks through X Ray machines, CCTVs (Close Circuit Television) for surveillance and inspections of the ship's hull, etc. Cruise line companies like the Royal Caribbean now hire contractors to provide intelligence and assist in devising risk management strategies.

Legal Aspects

If the maritime community is to effectively challenge the forces of terrorism, *it is imperative to establish a framework for a genuine link between the flag a vessel flies and the State it belongs to.*

On, 12 September 2002—The owner of a missing cargo of palm oil worth US $ 2.5 million was defeated in his court battle to recover insurance for the loss. The court in Hong Kong heard how analysis of the evidence suggested the cargo of polyolefin was the subject of a theft, well-planned and executed by the ship's fraudulent owners and operators.

In a ground-breaking move, the judge ruled that the cargo's insurers could not be held liable for the risks of the actual journey because it was different from the one described in the insurance policy.

The insurers' defence was based on a 100 year old maritime law, Section 44 of the Marine Insurance Act (MIA), which says a risk does not attach when a ship sets off for a destination other than that specified in the policy.

This was the first time that insurers have invoked Section 44 MIA to avoid paying up.

IMB Director Captain Pottengal Mukundan believes the Pacifica Judgement will significantly increase the pressure on traders worldwide to avoid dealing with unscrupulous shipping companies whose actions could threaten the validity of insurance policies to protect the cargo.

"This decision places a clear responsibility on cargo owners to make sure they check the viability of the ship owner and vessel before putting any cargo on board," said Captain Mukundan.

"It is now more important than ever for the cargo owner to check the credentials of all parties involved in a deal. It is often the case that the sellers choose a vessel under a CIF or CFR (Code of Federal Regulation) sale, but it is the buyers who hold title to the cargo, and face the financial loss after the vessel has disappeared. It is vital that in these circumstances buyers ensure that the choice of the vessel is subject to their approval."

According to Captain Mukundan, although phantom ship fraud is a sophisticated form of cargo theft, it is easy to avoid. He said, "IMBs information department maintains a database of current phantom ships and has helped many cargo owners avoid loading cargo on these criminal vessels. Once loaded, the chances of recovering the cargo are minimal."

ICC's International Maritime Bureau runs a due diligence service to help its members check the identity of all parties and vessels before entering into a contract. IMB is based in London, and as mentioned, runs the IMB Piracy Reporting Center in Kuala Lumpur.

Conclusion

In this chapter, a comprehensive analysis has been carried out of the existing State of Maritime Crime and the rising curve of piracy and terror. It is the gaping loop holes already provided by the existence of various types of maritime crime that opens up a huge window of vulnerability to the fleets of merchant ships, ports and maritime trade in general. The civil aviation industry has no such glaring loopholes. Hence, the need to plug these vulnerabilities in shipping provided by the extensive nature of maritime crime. Maritime crime provides the framework on which global terrorist networks could easily build up their operations. With the onset of mega terror, the potential of these crime networks is becoming ominous. The most worrying aspect is the emerging congruence between piracy and terrorism. The civil aviation industry is relatively much more secure. As of now, security is virtually non-existant in the maritime sector. When this vulnerability is contrasted with the gaping loopholes now being exploited by the networks of maritime crime, the serious threat to some 46000 merchant ships and over 4000 ports becomes patently obvious. Terroist incidents have already started on sea. Hijackings on sea are increasingly becoming more numerous. Many of the hijacking are in Indonesian territorial waters. "We are appealing to law enforcement agencies of the littoral states to keep a close watch on vessels in their own territorial waters, but particularly in the local hot spots such as Pulau Iyu Kecil. The lack of an effective law enforcement presence encourages the pirates to pursue their activities," Captain Mukundan, Director of the ICC IMB said.

The incidents of hijackings have increased dramatically since 2000," elaborated Captain Mukundun, "These are serious and violent attacks, committed by organized crime groups. Crewmembers are often abducted or injured and both ship and cargo worth millions of dollars are often stolen. The IMB calls upon the governments in South East Asia to ratify the SUA Convention of 1988, which will give them jurisdiction over these crimes when the vessels are recovered. The bombing of the French tanker, *VLCC Limberg* in Yemeni waters raises the specter of maritime terrorism against these extremely vulnerable vessels," Captain Mukundan added. "The IMB recommends that governments and port authorities consider prescribed traffic lanes for these vessels, where practicable, patrolled by Coast Guard vessels and kept free of all unauthorized craft."

He added: "The focused intelligence of the Piracy Reporting Center can be vital to resource-strapped law enforcement agencies for the optimum utilization of their resources.

According to Captain Mukundan, there is a greater than ever need to report piracy and increase awareness worldwide, as highly organized and resourced criminal networks move into the field, and attacks at sea become increasingly deadly.

Notes and References

(i)   ICC IMB *Annual Report 2001*, 'Piracy and Armed Robbery Against Ships', p.3

(ii) Ellen (1989), p.234

(iii) Lt. Cdr. R.C. Browbrick "Piracy : Ancient Myth or Modern Reality". *Naval Review*, Feb 2003 Issue Vol. 91. No. 1 (All bar chart graphs are based on IMO – International Piracy Reporting Center Data cited in the above article.

(iv) The United Nations Convention on the Law of the Sea (UNCLOS) lays down a comprehensive regime of law and order in the world's oceans and seas establishing rules governing all uses of the oceans and their resources. It enshrines the notion that all problems of ocean space are closely interrelated and need to be addressed as a whole. The Convention was opened for signature on December 10, 1982 in Montego Bay, Jamaica. The Convention entered into force in accordance with its Article 308 on November 16, 1994, 12 months after the date of deposit of the sixtieth instrument of ratification or accession. Today, it is the globally recognized regime dealing with all matters relating to the law of the sea. The Convention comprises 320 articles and nine annexes, governing all aspects of ocean space, such as delimitation, environmental control, marine scientific research, economic and commercial activities, transfer of technology and the settlement of disputes relating to ocean matters. For full text see: http://www.un.org/Depts/los/convention_agreements/texts/unclos/closindx.htm

1. "Organised Crime takes to High Seas", 4th Feb 2002 IMB *News Report.*

2. ICC IMB *Annual Report 2001*, 'Piracy and Armed Robbery Against Ships'.

3. "Landmark ruling mounts pressure against owners to avoid dealing with crooks", Hong Kong, 12 September 2002 IMB *News Report.*

4. "IMB investigates organised theft of cargo in Eastern Mediterranean" 17th Feb 2003, London, IMB *News Report.*

5. *Ibid.*

6. *Ibid.*

7. "What are FOCs: A brief guide to flags of convenience", www.itf.og.uk/seafarer/foc/body_foc.html

8. *Ibid.*

9. Paul Harris and Martin Bright, "How the armada of terror menaces Britain" *The Observer.* Sunday December 23, 2001,

10. Vijay Sakhuja

11. "IMB Calls For clamp-down on fake maritime documents", www.iccwbo.org/ccs/news_archives/2001/imb_fakes.asp

12. *Ibid.*

13. Paul Harris and Martin Bright, "How the armada of terror menaces Britain" *The Observer.* Sunday December 23, 2001,

14. Sophia Quentin, "Shipping Activities: Targets of Maritime Terrorism", *MIRMAL* ISSUE №2, 20-01-2003

15. *Ibid.*

16. "The Asymmetric Threat From Maritime terrorism", Jane's Navy International, October 2001, p.26.

17. Vijay Sakhuja

18. "Murky Flag-Of-Convenience Ship Registry System Could Hamper Effort To Uncover Terrorist Assets", www.amo-union.org/Newspaper/Morgue/11-2001/Sections/News/foc.html

19. Vijay Sakhuja

20. "The Asymmetric Threat From Maritime Terrorism'", *Jane's Navy International,* London, October 2001, p. 28.

21. "Renaissance Cruises Filing for Bankruptcy", www.seaview.co.uk/cruiselines/renaissance.

22. "Royal Caribbean, Princess to Merge", *The Los Angeles Times,* November 21, 2001.

23. See http://www.iccwbo.org/CCS/news_archives/2002

24. *Ibid.*

25. The PRC is financed by mariad companies. For example for the year 2003 the contributing firms included Britannia Steam Ship Insurance Association Limited, UK Fafalios Shipping S.A, Greece, Associazione Nazionale Fra Le Impresse Assicuratrici (ANIA), Italy GARD P&I, Norway International Operations S A, Athens Branch, Greece Japan P&I Club, Japan KG Projex-Schiffahrts GMBH, Hamburg, Germany Novorossiysk Shipping Company, RussiaOil Companies International Marine Forum (OCIMF), Petroships Private Ltd, Singapore, Reederei Nord Klaus E Oldendorff Ltd, Cyprus Samios Shipping Company S.A, Piraeus, Greece Seaarland Shipping Management Geselleschaft mbh, Austria, SKULD Standard Steamship Owners' Protection and Indemnity Association (Bermuda) Limited Limited TheThoresen and Company (Bangkok) Ltd, Thailand Union of Greek Ship owners, Greece United Arab Shipping Co SAG, Kuwait

26. Prem Vir Das

27. "Indian court jails pirates in breakthrough for marine security" Mumbai, India 25 February 2003, IMB *News Report*

28. Rahul Roy Choudhry

29. Stjepan Keckes, "Review of International Programmes relevant to the work of the independent World Commission on the Oceans", *draft report of the Independent World Commission on the Oceans, "The Ocean...Our Future",* 1998 p.15

30. Rahul Roy Choudhry " India's Maritime Security" *Knowledge World,* New Delhi Jun 2000.

◀3▶

Security on Sea

Beyond SOLAS

The rising graph of piracy and maritime crime had made it imperative that a comprehensive review of security procedures on sea be carried out urgently. A major impetus was given by the events of 9/11. As is well known, such security aspects were covered earlier by the International Convention on Safety of Life at Sea (SOLAS) which was promulgated in 1974. This was wholly inadequate for dealing with the highly enlarged and altered context provided by piracy and the growing menace of terrorism.

ISPS Code

Following the tragic events of 11 Sep 2001, the 22nd Session of the Assembly of the International Maritime Organisation in Nov 2001, unanimously agreed to the development of new measures relating to security of ships and port facilities.[1] These were to be adopted by a Conference of Contracting Governments to the International Convention for the Safety of Life at Sea (1974). Preparatory work for the Conference was entrusted to the Organisations Maritime Security Committee (MSC) on the basis of submissions made by member states, inter governmental organisations and Non Governmental Organisations (NGOs) in consultation with the organisation.[2] To expedite issues, the MSC in turn established an MSC Intersessional Working Group on Maritime Security which held its first meeting in Feb 2002. In March 2002, the 75th session of the MSC considered these proposals and an adhoc working group was established to further refine and develop these. Further meetings of the MSC were held. Finally, the Diplomatic Conference on Maritime Security took place in London from 09 – 13 Dec 2002. This conference adopted the amendments to the existing SOLAS convention (SOLAS 74).[3] It decided to accelerate the implementation of the following:-

(a) Installation of Automatic Identification System (AIS) in ships.
(b) New Regulations in Chapter XI-I of SOLAS 74 covering marking of the Ship Identification Numbers.
(c) Carriage of a Continuous Synopsis Record.[4]

The Conference also agreed to follow up the co-operative work with the International Labour Organisation. (ILO) and World Customs Organisation (WCO). The provision of Chapter XI-2 of SOLAS 74 and this code apply to ships and ports facilities. However, it was agreed that provisions relating to port facilities should relate solely to the ship/port interface. The wider issue of the Security of the port area will be the subject of further joint work between the International Maritime Organization and the ILO.[5]

Implementation of these provisions will require effective continuing cooperation and understanding between the ships personnel, port personnel, passengers, cargo interests, ships and port management and those in National and Local Authorities with Security responsibilities. Part B of this Code provides guidance for implementing the Security Provisions set out in Chapter XI-2 of SOLAS 74.[6] *The International Code for Security of Ships and Port Facilities* (or the ISPS

Code) therefore is the New Bible for Security at Sea in the face of enhanced threats posed by Piracy, Maritime crime and Terrorism.

Objectives

Broadly the objectives of this code are :-

- To establish an international framework for co-operation between govts, Govt. agencies, local administrations and shipping and port industries to detect security threats and take preventive measures against security incidents affecting ships and port facilities used in international trade.

- To establish respective roles and responsibilities of the various agencies involved in the above.

- To ensure early and efficient collection and exchange of security-related information.

- To provide a methodology for security assessments.

- To ensure confidence that adequate and proportionate maritime security measures are in place.[7]

Functional Requirements

To achieve these objectives the code envisages a number of functional requirements such as :-

- Gathering and assessing information with respect to security threats and exchanging such information with the Govts.

- The maintenance of communications protocols for ships and port facilities.

- Preventing unauthorised access to ships, port facilities and their restricted areas.

- Preventing the introduction of unauthorised weapons incendiary devices or explosives to ships or port facilities.

- Providing means for raising the alarm in reaction to security threats and security incidents.

- Requiring ships and port facilities to prepare security plans based upon an assessment of threats.

- Requiring ships and port authorities to carry out regular training, drills and exercises to ensure familiarity with security plans and procedures.

In consonance with these, the new code requires the appointment of Company Security Officer and Ship Security Officers who draw up Ship Security Plans and procedures. The code delineates three levels of security alert (namely Security Levels 1,2 and 3 etc.). It also stipulates the appointment of Port Security Officers and the preparation and implementation of Port Security Plans.[8]

Terrorist Risk Factors

The US Maritime Transport Committee in its Report of Jul 2003 entitled "Security in Maritime Transport" has highlighted the Risk Factors that originate from Terrorism.[9] These can broadly be grouped under five heads as under:-

- Cargo
- People
- External Impacts
- Money
- Vessels

Cargo: Most of the worlds non bulk cargo travels in marine shipping containers. A fleet of 2700 modular container vessels and the emergence of a global network of over 430 highly automated ports handling facilities had revolutionised the transport of goods by sea. A total of 232 million containers were moved through container ports in 2001. This system is porous enough and can easily be subverted.[10]

- Containers could be used to conceal and deliver relatively crude Weapons of Mass Destruction (WMD).
- It could be used to smuggle in people/weapons/small arms and explosives.
- Additional cost of transport due to additional security measures and its adverse impact on general economics.

People: This aspect has been covered in detail in the Chapter on Maritime Crime. Terrorist groups could infiltrate ship crews. The basic threats would be :-

(a) Smuggle people/weapons on board ships.

(b) Use Cargo to transport Conventional, Nuclear, Chemical or Biological Weapons.[11]

External Factors: Terrorism has a major impact on the external factors relating to maritime trading activities. In specific these relate to :-

- Loss of life and damage to property directly effects confidence in merchant shipping and its security.
- Terrorist attacks could severly disrupt trade flows and cause a serious set back to the global economy.
- Additional cost of transport due to enhanced security measures could seriously raise the cost of exports/imports and hurt global trade by reducing margins of profit and/ or substantially hiking up prices of such goods.[12]

Money: This can take two forms:-

- Using revenue from shipping to fund terrorist activities. Thus, the LTTE has a fleet of 10-12 ships under flags of convenience which usually carries innocent cargo to earn money (Hard board, coconuts etc.) but can also be used for smuggling of arms, and narcotics.
- Use ships to launder illicit funds for terrorist organisations.[13]

Vessels: These are the prime targets of terrorist attacks on sea. Today, there are approximately 46,000 merchant ships in the world. The terrorists could :-

- Use the Vessels as weapons on the analogy of the civil aviation strikes of 9/11. Oil Tankers (V.L.C.C) would be particularly vulnerable to such exploitation.

- Sinking Vessels to disrupt infrastructure – by blocking fairways in ports or sinking large vessels in critical choke points like the Straits of Malacca etc.

Let us now focus mainly on the Security of Ships.[14]

Analysis of Threat/Attack Profiles

Each ship will need to evolve and practice its own Security Plan. However, an analysis of general threat profiles will be essential to arrive at the specific counter measures/ response procedures.

Terrorist threat Profile

The Terrorist attack profile is best reconstructed by recapitulating the case studies of actual terrorist attacks conducted so far. In chronological sequence these are :-

- **1961** Political insurgents had embarked on and seized Portuguese Passenger Ship *Santa Maria*. The plan was to hijack the vessel and take it to Spanish Guinea and Angola.

- **1985** Four Palestine Liberation Front (PLF) terrorists hijacked the Italian liner *Achille Lauro* carrying over 400 passengers and crew off Egypt. Terrorists demanded release of imprisoned colleagues in Israel and killed a disabled American tourist. After a two day drama, the hijackers surrendered on assurance of safe passage.

- **1989** Three terrorists of Abu Nidal Organisation boarded Greek Cruise ferry *City of Poros* with 500 passengers. They opened fire and threw grenades killing 9 and wounded 100 people. Plan was to hold passengers hostage.

- **Oct 2000** A small craft carrying explosives pulled up alongside *USS Cole* (an Arleigh Burke Class destroyer) while it was refueling outside Yemen Harbour. Ship was seriously damaged by explosion which also caused casualties to the crew. The explosives were carried in a small boat that came up alongside the ship undetected.

- **Oct 2002** French Tanker *MT Limburg* was similarly attacked by a Fiber Glass speed boat carrying explosives which blew an 8 by 11 meter hole in its hull in Yemen territorial waters.

Thus terrorist attack profiles so far have focused on two general methodologies :-

- Armed terrorists boarding passenger ships and trying to hijack the ship and kill/take hostage the crew and passengers.

- Small boats laden with explosives blowing up hulls of warship/oil tankers by sneaking up to the ship undetected.

Basic counter measures Against this typology of terrorist attacks, the basic counter measures would be :-

- **Access Control** Thorough and comprehensive check of passengers and personnel boarding ship at port and the use of hand held and door frame metal detectors to locate weapons/explosives. Sniffer dogs at embarkation ports can also be usefully employed.

- **Need for Radar and Additional Crew Watches** In both the cases of the *USS Cole* and *MT Limburg*, there was need for more focused radar scanning and extra watches to detect small boats approaching the target ships. Early detection can lead to effective safety measures, like flood lighting, warning on loud hailers and evasion maneuvers. Levels of security alerts in such areas (e.g. Coast of Yemen) have to be specifically enhanced.

- Port Authorities should have prescribed traffic lanes for Very Large Crude Carriers (V.L.C.C) and other vulnerable

Vessels. (e.g LNG Carriers, Nuclear Waste Carriers etc.). These should be actively patrolled by Coast Guard Vessels and helicopters and kept free of all unauthorised traffic. In periods of very high threat, or on reciept of specific intelligence, such vessels could be provided Coast Guard Vessels, escorts while entering sensitive Ports or sealanes that lie close to hostile activity shores (Coast of Yemen, Somalia, Straits of Malacca etc.).

Pirate Attack Profiles

Chapter 2 contains a detailed statistical and graphical analysis of the piracy attack profiles since 1994. These invariably involve :-

- Pirate Vessels commonly follow a parallel course to potential target but generally at a distance of a few cables (so that they can not be seen visually). Then they close upto about two cables astern to observe the ship and determine if it is easy target. If pirates decide to attack a vessel, they are likely to approach at very high speed.

- Boarding the ship in harbour or via grapnels and lines thrown in coastal waters by pirates in smaller craft.

- Use of knives is increasingly giving way to use of fire arms.

- The decreasing ratio of attempted boarding to successful boardings does indicate that crew alertness and piracy watches have proved successful in staving off such attacks.

The prime methodology for countering pirate attacks is enhanced alertness in susceptible waters. Prevention is better than cure. The commercial ships sole chance lies in early detection and prevention of embarkation/boarding. Alert crews can easily foil such attempts. The radar operator should announce the compass direction of the target. The ship if moving should increase speed and alter course to seawards if possible.

- On detection of such attempts use search lights, whistles, and water hoses to defeat the attempted boarding.

- Use of fire arms or Ship Marshals has not been considered viable or advisable.

- However, electric fences on ships which give a non-lethal shock of some 9000 volts are a futuristic system which holds much promise.

- Non-lethal sprays which make boarding ropes/cables highly slippery would also be a viable option.

- Search lights can be used to blind or dazzle the pirates and water hoses can be used to defeat any attempt to board using grapnels and lines. If grapnel hooks are used, cut the attached lines.

- Prevention is better than cure. In such waters it is imperative that ships maintain constant visual and radar search for small craft. The crews must be alerted to maintain a high state of vigilance. 24 hours visual and security watches will have to be kept in such locations. It would be advisable to choose anchorages away from fairways.

Terrorist/Piratic attack profiles are not likely to remain constant. In fact, these are likely to be dynamic and constantly changing. New attack profiles could include :-

- Exploiting Containers to transport Weapons of Mass Destruction (e.g. Radiological Dispersal Devices – RDDs or Biological or Chemical agents), arms and explosives and even infiltrate armed personnel.

- Hijacking huge cargo ships or tankers to use them as battering rams against Ports/Jetties/ other ships.

- Sinking hijacked ships in critical choke points or narrow channels – e.g. Malacca Straits etc. Post 9/11 the United States Coast Guard now provides armed escorts to cargo ships entering harbour-with officers from the Coast Guard going aboard, securing the engine room and bridge, screening crew members and cargo. Cruise ships are even more carefully guarded. They get armed escorts and no other ships are allowed to move as they enter harbour. Armed ships berth on either side once they dock.

• Deploying plastic explosives on sensitive/vulnerable points on the vessel-evading detection by resorting to unconventional methods including under water diving, aerial attacks, stealth and wolf pack tactics etc.

To deal with this enhanced/enlarged threat profile, we will have to exploit/leverage technology. In Chapter 7, a very comprehensive survey of new technologies that can assist the shipping industry in this field, has been carried out. Some key technologies are :-

• Ship Tracking and Electronic Notification of Vessels.

• Video Surveillance Equipment.

• Electronic Fencing.

• Biometric Assisted Identification.

• Radiation Isotope Identification Devices.

• Electronic Seals for checking tampering of Containers.

• Powerful Radiation Sensors on Cranes and Mobile Drive through portals with X Rays and Geiger Sensors etc.

Containers: As highlighted in earlier chapters, containers are a key vulnerability. There are various types of Containers designed to accommodate different needs : dry-van (closed), open-top, open-side, bulk, flatrack, tank, refrigerated and others. The most common sizes are of normal 20 feet and 40 feet lengths as set forth in the various specifications for International Organisation for Standardisation (ISO). These constitute the prime vectors for infiltrating personnel, explosives, WMD on board ships. Most common concealment measures would be false frontwalls or built up floors, false cielings, enclosed exterior bottoms and in container frames. Refrigerated containers are particularly vulnerable. Trailers of containers can also be used to conceal contraband. Careful documentation is a vital aspect. All containers and trailers will have to be inspected very thoroughly. This aspect will be covered in much greater detail in the next chapter.

The credentials of seamen is a major issue. As per the ISPS code, Issue of verifiable seamen identification had to be completed by Jun 03. This is a critical area as a very large number of sea men are recruited from Indonesia and Philippines – areas of the rising ideological influence of the Al Qaida and other extremist fundamentalist groups. The other most worrisome issue is the Flags of Convenience, which could easily facilitate terrorist/piratic fleets for carrying of arms and explosives and narcotics.

Notes

1. International Ship and Port Facility Security Code and SOLAS Amendments 2002. Bhandarkar Publications, Mumbai. 2003 Edition.
2. *Ibid.*
3. *Ibid.*
4. *Ibid.*
5. *Ibid.*
6. *Ibid.*
7. *Ibid.*
8. *Ibid.*
9. US Maritime Transport Committee Report of July 2003. (Prepared for Organisation for Economic Co-operation and Development).
10. *Ibid.*
11. *Ibid.*
12. *Ibid.*
13. *Ibid.*
14. *Ibid.*

◀4▶

Port and Trade Security Issues

Weak link: Compromised Port Security

Maritime shipping is bound to be the next frontier in the war on terrorism, and the soft underbelly might not be just the sea borne traffic but the sea ports that are the hubs of commerce for any maritime nation. Any measure of real security has been sacrificed in the quest for speed and economy on the world's oceans, and addressing the major issues has been labeled a daunting task. World trade is expected to double in 20 years and triple in 50 years, and ports need more money to pay for security improvements and expansion.

There is therefore, a serious need to identify and react to the challenges and risks present in a serious and organized manner. 9/11 has brought the issue of port security into very sharp focus in the USA. There have been a series of very informative articles in the *New York Times,* the *Tribune* and the *Observer* newspapers and many articles on the internet that throw considerable light on this vital subject. In this chapter, a wide array of sources have been tapped to collate the various measures and initiatives that have been undertaken in the USA. These are extremely educative and merit detailed study and analysis on our part.

There is no doubt that in this field there has to be international co-operation and a common framework for sharing information / intelligence and combined measures taken to mitigate and deter all terrorist threats and activities related to shipping.

Shipping Unions say that the systems of controls for the international merchant shipping fleet was ripe for abuse by the terrorists. It has got to do with the way the shipping industry regulates itself. It is a murky world of corruption, bribes, lawlessness and Flags of Convenience.

'A lot of the industry itself is based on quite a lot of corruption and deceit that fosters anonymity and allows unscrupulous operators,' says Andrew Linnington of the National Union of Marine Aviation and Shipping Transport Officers in the United States.

The world's largest fleets belong to the Bahamas, Panama and Liberia. Liberia alone maintains a fleet of 1,557, despite the fact that it is a country devastated by civil war with a barely functioning infrastructure. But, of course, the ships are registered on paper only. That allows them to avoid taxes and other costs and lines the pockets of corrupt port officials. Tiny island nations, such as the Marshall Islands and St Vincent & the Grenadines, also maintain huge registries, having fleets much bigger than Britain or the United States.

Industry sources also point to the practice of 'flag-hopping', whereby ships will be taken off the registry of one country at the first signs of a crackdown by authorities and re-registered under a different flag with no threat.[1]

The laxity of seaports has been an open secret amongst the smugglers. For decades they have used small boats and shipping containers for transporting narcotics. In the

Mumbai bomb blasts in 1993 and 2003 the explosives were mostly inducted by small boats operated by smugglers. Criminals have in the past succeeded in circumventing legislated security measures.

A case reported by the IMB highlights how easily port security can be compromised by resourceful criminals, and worse, terrorists. This forms an instructive case study.

A theft occurred at a warehouse within a secured port area. Prior to loading, container seals and contents were properly checked and the required paperwork completed.

Later, workers within the warehouse tipped off the thieves, pointing them to the location of those containers holding high value cargo. In this case, the heist involved cigarettes. It is assumed that that personnel manning the gate also assisted the thieves, as they were able to drive in and out of the compound unimpeded.

While still within the port area, the container seals were carefully removed and the contents extracted. The seals were then replaced and the original, now empty, containers were returned to the warehouse. While it was noted that the containers were no longer in their original order, no action was taken to determine how or why this occurred. The container seal numbers were checked against the manifest before loading, but there was no further scrutiny.

On arrival at their destination, the containers were opened and found to be empty. The consignor immediately claimed the ships' crew must have heisted the cargo en-route, as the paperwork showed no irregularities at the loading port. The company concerned is said to be currently pursuing a claim against the carrier to recover the loss.[2]

To complicate matters further, measures taken to secure major ports and adjacent military installations are not a panacea in themselves but attention also needs to be given to scores of privately owned facilities which dot the waterfront of the maritime states. Coal piers, grain piers, rail hubs, wharves, repair berths and other non-containerized cargo facilities sit exposed with no concerted plan or centralised way to monitor their security against intruders. Where there is maritime legislation requiring private companies to implement security plans, little financial assistance is available to help businesses meet those goals.

Beefing up

There is a need for a series of security enhancements including addition of video surveillance equipment, electronic fencing, high-tech lighting equipment, harbour surveillance systems, underwater detection systems, Radio isotope identification devices, specialized surveillance vessels, smart identification cards - biometrics and information security technologies etc.

Resources available will have to be ascertained and deficiencies quickly catered for. Increasing police personnel, checking their backgrounds, setting new training standards and establishing an effective command-control-communication(C3) system are called for. An assessment of port vulnerability should be done and security models, plans and guidelines formulated, applied and regular monitoring and upgradation must be carried out. While the government or the administration is responsible, the scope of security needs will require inputs from the Coast Guard, port authorities, Navy, local law enforcement and local maritime businesses. As security experts point out, there should be Intelligence sharing amongst security agencies and international partners and defensive parameters should be set by the security agencies ideally well outside the port area i.e. as seawards as possible.

How real is the threat?

Post 9/11 there have been speculations regarding likely targets of terror strikes. Earlier, terrorist strikes conjured up images of a fanatic group targeting an important building, the masses, public transports and the like. With 9/11 demonstrating the modern terrorist mind's ingenuity, determination and technical knowledge, it is increasingly clear and infact logical, that a port offers maximum vulnerability with the most far reaching consequences. Intrusion through sea by any means by undetected small boats, diving/underwater activity, container boxes, highjacked merchant vessels etc. is far more easier to achieve and thus *singles it out as the most penetrable environment* taking into consideration the ignorance and lack of security standards of the facilities and public at large.

Coupled with exsisting evils of the industry like piracy, maritime crime, FOC, poor detection of container contents, low security standards and accountability along the whole transport chain lends it susceptible to organised terrorist attacks.

Potential Fifth Horsemen? Anatomy of an Apocalypse

The attack on a port could be delivered by means of a vessel carrying explosives, a huge ship with a cargo of oil/gas or a container shipped in carrying WMDs (Weapons of Mass Destruction), RDDs (Radiological Dispersal Devices) or crude "dirty" bombs. Would Osama Bin Laden be interested? Recent reports seem to suggest that its not merely a probability – it's a fact. Is it possible that a container carrying a WMD be shipped right into a city without ever being detected?

Shipping experts say just two percent of shipping containers entering the U.S. are inspected. The weakness of the inspection regime is illustrated by U.S. Drug Enforcement Agency estimates that about 90 percent of cocaine shipments to the U.S. get through undetected.[3]

"Virtually every time a ship docks, the only people who know what is on a container are the people who shipped it and the people picking it up," said U.S. Senator Dianne Feinstein, D-California, during testimony before a Presidential Commission last year. "And if those people are terrorists, they are free to ship munitions and weapons overseas to their compatriots or even set off a bomb."

As regards containers, only a few are examined for their contents. According to maritime security experts, containers are the most suitable means of transporting men and material for terrorist activities, including weapons of mass destruction. For instance, in New Orleans, a container labeled as empty held oil exploration tools that were radioactive. When customs officials opened the container in the port, beeper-size radiation alarms on their belts screamed a warning. The inspectors had to summon a de-contamination team.[4] Containers have been used in the past to transport humans.

Inspectors in Italy found a suspected Al-Qaida terrorist hiding in a shipping container equipped with a bed and makeshift bathroom. The suspect, an Egyptian in a business suit, had with him a Canadian passport, a laptop computer, two cell phones, airport maps, security passes for airports in three countries and a certificate proclaiming him an airplane mechanic. The container was headed for Toronto.[5] He was later released due to lack of evidence for implicating him in any sort of terrorist activity.

Osama Bin Laden maintains a secret shipping fleet flying a variety of flags of convenience, allowing him to hide his ownership and transport goods, arms, drugs and recruits with little official scrutiny, according to recent reports and court testimony. In 1998, one of Bin Laden's cargo freighters unloaded supplies in Kenya for the suicide bombers who weeks later destroyed the U.S. embassies in Kenya and Tanzania.[6]

British, US and European intelligence services have been desperately searching for Bin Laden's 'phantom fleet' amid fears that the vessels could be carrying poisons, explosives or weapons.

The ships were identified as a result of a joint intelligence operation thought to be led by the Norwegian security service and America's CIA with the help of international shipping registries. The search has been hampered by the controversial 'flags of convenience' system, under which many ships are registered as Panamanian, Liberian or Cypriot to avoid stringent checks on their crews and cargoes.[7]

British anti-terrorist officers searched the London-bound *MV Nisha*, seized off the south coast of England in a dramatic raid by Royal Navy units, including the Special Boat Service (SBS). The ship, which lay off Sandown Bay in the Isle of Wight, was flying the flag of St Vincent and the Grenadines, in the West Indies. The tiny Caribbean nation has a population of just 111,000, but 1,336 vessels fly its flag. The dawn raid on the ship by the SBS and the Metropolitan Police Special Branch came after the tip off from a foreign Intelligence service that a ship like the *Nisha*, carrying explosives, was due to dock in London.

Shipping experts have expressed fears about the vulnerability of targets in the City of London to attack from the river. *The Nisha* would have passed Canary Wharf, the capital's highest building.[8]

Spies across the world are hunting the world's oceans for the flotilla of terror ships .They have been looking for them since the end of September, working closely with international maritime organisations and scouring log books and cargo registers to try to trace their movements. The ships' names are known, but have not yet been disclosed out of a fear of forcing them into hiding.

Does Osama Bin Laden have the capability to assemble a crude bomb?

Near Kandahar in Southern Afghanistan, Uranium and Cyanide have reportedly been discovered in drums at an Al-Qaida terrorist base. The *London Telegraph* said that the find — the first evidence that terrorist mastermind Osama Bin Laden had obtained materials for a nuclear arsenal — was confirmed by U.S. officials. The cache included a low-grade Uranium which could be used to make a so-called "dirty bomb," or a crude radiological device wrapped around a conventional explosive. Such a bomb is designed to spread radiation over a large area after exploding.[9]

The CIA reportedly told the (U.S.) President at one point of not only the published arrests by Pakistan of two former nuclear scientists who visited terrorist mastermind Osama Bin Laden, but of a third Pakistani scientist who tried to sell a nuclear bomb to Libya. The likeliest source for terrorists of nuclear materials was the crumbling nuclear industry infrastructure in parts of the former Soviet Union, despite the insistence of Russian officials that all such materials are accounted for.[10] However in recent times one of the most likely source of nuclear material for terrorists is from Pakistan. Dr A.Q. Khan laboratories of Pakistan have been implicated in supply of nuclear material and know how to North Korea, Iran and Libya. Some

Pakistani Nuclear Scientists who were part of a so called charitable organisation called Tamier-e-Nau had reportedly met Osama Bin Laden in Afghanistan. While a suticase nuclear bommb may be beyond the capabilities of terrorist organisations, most Counter-terrorism experts point out that they could easily assemble Radiological-Dispersal Devices (RDD) or crude dirty bombs.

Such devices could explode conventional high explosives to spread industrial, medical-grade or waste radioactive material into a populated area, in an effort to cause panic and provoke a widespread fear of exposure. Such an explosion, detonated by terrorists, could necessitate evacuation and decontamination of the area and probably disrupt a local economy for a long period of time.

A war games exercise sponsored by Booz Allen Hamilton of Washington, D.C., simulated what would happen if terrorists unleashed dirty bombs. The conclusion: U.S. ports

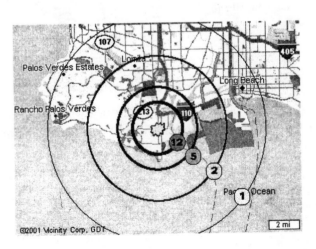

The temple above depicts pressure damage calculations based on a one Megaton surface detonation on a port.

would shut down for more than a week, with a direct loss to the nation's economy of $58 billion.[11]

The employment of a standard nuclear bomb on a port installation gives some idea of the damage that a nuclear device could cause. It also gives an idea of what an RDD could do.

This diagram depicts possible fallout patterns based on prevailing westerly winds. These calculations are based on

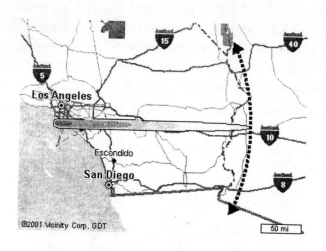

a one Megaton blast. This simulation exercise is based upon a nuclear device being used on the American port of Los Angles.

The Tosco Refinery/Tank Farm is located at Ground Zero. The explosive nature of the refinery has not been factored in to the blast assessment

The pictures depict the Mobil Southwestern Terminal and West way Petrol-Chemical Tank Farms located adjacent to Ground Zero. The explosive nature of the contents of the storage tanks has not been ascertained.

Installations like these could greatly compound the level of damage and enlarge the magnitude of the resultant disaster.

Targets for such attacks would be cities where large residential areas are near to docks, ideally docks that carry gas or oil. Cities that fit the bill could include Boston, which has a large liquid natural gas trade, San Francisco and Sydney. Despite the bridges across the Thames, London would also be vulnerable as large ships could easily penetrate as far as Canary Wharf - which has been the target of IRA terrorist attacks. Terrorism experts believe the ships could even be fitted with primitive radioactive 'dirty bombs' or hijackers could take over boats carrying nuclear or chemical waste. If hijackers took over a small private yacht it would be unlikely to come to the attention of the authorities. It, too, could be turned into a floating bomb and piloted down rivers or through docks and into large Western cities.

Despite US naval patrols stopping traffic in the Mediterranean and Arabian waters, such crafts could easily evade capture. They are already widely used by international drug-smuggling rings and other criminal organisations. Piracy is also endemic and on the rise. That raises the real possibility that Al-Qaida cells would not have to infiltrate a crew, but could simply hijack the boat, take it over and steer it to their target. It would be a grim water-borne mirror image of the hijacked planes crashing into New York and the Pentagon.

A recent audiotape believed to have been made by Osama Bin Laden praised and seemed to take responsibility for a suicide attack in which a speedboat packed with explosives rammed and crippled a French tanker, *the Limburg*, off Yemen. Other leaders of Al Qaida have vowed to cut the "economic lifelines" of the world's industrialized societies. The threats have focused the attention of Intelligence agencies and marine police worldwide on the vulnerability of tankers. Representatives of most of the world's seagoing nations met in London to discuss how to keep ships safe from the long-term problem of piracy and the new risks of terrorism.[12]

From reports of theft of radioactive material used in leakage detection of oil pipelines in Nigeria, to experiments in anthrax and bio terrorism methods - all could tomorrow be a part of a multistage heist to smuggle in WMD from the sea, right through a sensitive port node, up the energy commerce life lines and into the heart of a nation.

Current Awareness and Response Scenario

Of late, most maritime powers have begun to examine potential threats and draft initiatives to be undertaken to minimize such risks. In totality though, the response is not yet adequate to contain the variety of permutations and combinations of infiltration through the maritime commerce setup available. All initiatives will in any case consume a certain time period before the measures are fully established. The interim period between the promulgation and commencement of such measures is substantial enough to witness a major terrorist strike.

Hence, instead of waiting for a state sponsored measure or an international legislation to come into force, and coax all affected into conformity, all possible measures to establish effective security must be undertaken by all parties involved in marine transport and commerce. Grants and short term measures to encourage these may be provided as these would prove beneficial in the long run, even if not affording optimal organisation and effectiveness on an immediate basis.

The most likely target still remains the United States of America and it would be worthwhile to discuss in brief some of the latest measures being undertaken in the U.S. and by the International community. Other Countries very high on the list for possible terrorist strikes are Israel, India and UK.

Post 9/11 scenario in the U.S. – Homeland Security Initiatives

Within the United States itself, there has been a call for federal funding echoed by the American Association of Port Authorities as Federal grants/ similar measures could help offset some of the major costs incurred during a series of security enhancements. It was in fact argued that the costs of enhanced Security would be miniscule when compared to the damage mega-terror strikes on US ports could inflict on the American and global economy.

It was seen that there was an increasing need to put together a plan that met the objectives of the security requirements while not impeding the flow of commerce. In recent years officials at ports had resisted any uniform federal standards for security. Tougher stands got softened in an effort to protect commerce. No minimum standards for security plans had been set, there was further need to set policies, draft security guidelines, shore up funding and provide a comprehensive security guide for the services firms.

It was felt that as America scrambled to secure airports against terrorists, it was neglecting the nations most vulnerable gateways - its 361 ports. It was subsequently realised and in the words of Commandant Admiral James Loy, who addressed the IMO,"We must change our assumptions underlying maritime security. What we saw on September 11 was new ... hijackers taking over commercial flights for the sole purpose of turning them into human guided weapons of mass destruction. We must translate that thought pattern and *recognize the vulnerability of our maritime environment."*

Maritime security experts warned that U.S. coastal cities are wide open to attack from the sea. Fuel-laden tankers could be seized and used as floating missiles, or any one of tens of thousands of shipping containers shuttled into the country each day could contain a terrorist chemical, biological, or nuclear device.

The United States relies heavily on shipping to import almost 50 percent of the 19.5 million barrels of oil it consumes each day, and to carry nearly all of the 90 million tons of grain it exports each year.[13]

In general, the Coast Guard patrols the waterways, the U.S. Customs Service spot-checks international cargo and the Immigration and Naturalization Service reviews the visa status of cruise-ship passengers and crews. The local port authorities serve mainly as landlords, leasing out terminals to private companies. One Florida port official compared the arrangement to a shopping mall, where mall security polices public space and each store provides its own security.[14]

The U.S. Immigration and Naturalization Service is trying to recover from several security failures, including many in Hampton Roads in 2002. [15] Port security experts say lax security checkpoints at shore present a larger and more pervasive threat. The Norfolk office of the Immigration and Naturalization Service (INS) in 2002 allowed 40 crews from foreign cargo vessels to go ashore without proper authorization. In one instance, four Pakistani men disappeared after going ashore from the cargo ship *Progresso*, touching off a nationwide manhunt. That incident also led to reorganization at the Norfolk office of INS, also now part of the Federal Homeland Security Department.[16]

Customs is getting into the act much sooner. For example, Customs officials inspect some U.S.-bound cargoes in Rotterdam, Amsterdam, sealing the containers electronically. Global positioning systems enable officials to detect when the electronic seals are broken. The system is expensive, but it works.[17]

Concerns were growing that the Coast Guard - the chief line of defence – was getting overstretched and under funded. On 10 September, the day before the terrorist attacks on New York City and the Pentagon, the U.S. Coast Guard spent one percent of its operating budget on maritime and port security. In end 2001 it spent 57 percent. That shows the magnitude of the change.[18]

Since 11 September, the USCG has increased its patrols of "critical national infrastructure", such as ports, oil terminals and coastal nuclear power stations around the country, activating 2,700 reservists nationwide. *Cargo ships entering some of the harbours are given an armed escort, with officers from the Port and the Coast Guard going aboard, securing the engine room and bridge, screening crew members and spot-checking cargo.* Even more attention is paid to cruise ships.

Vessels calling at the port also have to provide 96 hours' notice of their arrival, up from 24 hours, and ships must notify the Coast Guard 30 minutes before reaching its jurisdictional limit, which extends 12 miles out to sea. Information about each vessel's crew and cargo is coordinated through the National Vessel Movement Center, a Coast Guard operation in Martinsburg, W. Va.[19]

Records indicate that before 9/11, the threat of terrorism was considered remote. In the previous nine years, the Puget Sound Coast Guard repeatedly inspected companies at seven ports and two oil refineries, and issued only four formal citations for security violations. Since the Sept. 11 attacks, the Coast Guard looked again at security plans for those facilities and cited 30 of them as deficient.[20]

The overstretched U.S. Coast Guard, on an average, inspected a port facility only once every two years.

Prior to 9-11, the Coast Guard station focused mainly on rescue efforts, education and the enforcement of boating-safety laws, routine safety inspections etc. now, the Guard has stepped up enforcement and intelligence-gathering activities, mainly because it is now part of the Federal Office of Homeland Security. Since then it has received further assistance in improving its available resources, for example, The Navy has provided the local Guard station with about $250,000 worth of radar and camera equipment for a jerry-rigged harbour surveillance system, which observes the harbour of the Chesapeake

Bay.[21] *The U.S. Navy has also detached a 13 warship-contingent for use by the Coast Guard.*

The USCG has played an active role to step up security measures and has provided the impetus - as well as some of the finance-for negotiations to tighten global maritime security, and as with the broader war on terror, it has been strongly backed.

Port authorities have also now acknowledged the viability of the threats and taken further initiatives which had been hitherto ignored. There is very much a business mindset at the U.S. ports, but now its being assimilated that the State itself is not the sole responsible agent of change. It is increasingly recognised that private companies provide the front-line defence against trouble in the U.S.

In 1999, a special Presidential Commission looked at 12 seaports around the country, and found alarming inadequacies. Those included unfenced cargo yards, poorly trained security guards and insufficient standards for workers with access to sensitive areas.[22]

Most port operators did not fulfill their obligations. Port security was often focused on preventing goods leaving a port rather than preventing unauthorized people and their weapons getting to the ship. In many ports, access to a ship was completely open, and in some cases port authorities even insisted that this was a traditional right of their citizens. When security was requested by ship owners, this was seen to be an opportunity to make money. Invoices were produced to provide restricted areas, access checks and searching.

Terminal operators, usually shipping companies, determined the number, qualifications and pay of the security guards they hired. *Operators were subsequently required by federal law to file security plans with the local U.S. Coast Guard office, which could order changes and fine or shut down those that didn't comply.* Some ports, such as Los Angeles and Port Everglades in Florida, considered requiring their tenants to provide better security before leases were renewed, as perception of the threat and active participation increased and trickled down to lower (and passive) levels of the maritime setup.

The L.A. port's Operations Director, Cunningham, said the stringent measures imposed there were worth the cost and the inconvenience, and were ultimately good for business.

Major ports around the country have spruced up their security and screening levels. Maximum use of new available technologies has been sought as evidenced by some of the latest measures implemented by certain ports – cited below.

The port of Los Angeles has taken an aggressive posture toward security.

"Our biggest target for terrorism is our passenger-cruise terminal," said Noel Cunningham, Operations Director and the port's former Chief of Police. Cruise ships are essentially floating hotels, with as many as 5,000 passengers densely packed in a steel-plated shell. At a port or in a shipping lane, suicide terrorists using a small, fast boat laden with explosives could quickly tie up at a ship near its vast fuel tanks and ignite a holocaust. "A successful terrorist attack on any one of these ships could result in a catastrophic number of casualties and threaten the economic viability of the entire industry," said Coast Guard Commandant Adm. James M. Loy. In Los Angeles, *cruise ships get armed escorts into harbour. While they are approaching the port, no other ships are allowed to move. And once docked, they are flanked by Coast Guard and police boats.*[23]

Hampton Roads is the second largest port on the U.S. East Coast, handling more than a million cargo containers each year, with more than $30 billion in cargo crossing its docks. Goods include everything from potato chips to blue jeans to Chinese-made merchandise. Hampton Roads' economy depends heavily on port commerce: more than 2,200 local residents work at the port. Hundreds more work at jobs for private port-related services companies in the Tidewater region. Only a few hundred yards away from the wharves is the Norfolk Naval Base. It is the largest naval facility in the U.S and comprises of every type of warship, including nuclear-powered aircraft carriers and submarines that are playing decisive roles in the wars against terrorism and Iraq. "We are the most target-rich port in the U.S.," says Robert Merhige, Deputy Executive Director and General Counsel for the Virginia Port Authority (VPA), which manages Virginia's publicly owned marine ports and facilities. To guard against bombs designed to spew radioactive waste in the middle of the port and put much of the U.S. Atlantic Fleet's Headquarters out of action, the Hampton Roads port installed the first radiation-detection system in the country.[24]

Onshore, VPA uses sophisticated technology to keep tabs on what's in containers passing through the port. Standing guard on the VPA wharves is a port police officer. As each truck rig straddles the $100,000 machinery, a Radiation Isotope Identification Device (RIID), the officer checks the results on a special monitor to collect images and gauges to indicate if isotopes are escaping and anything is suspicious. If the reading exceeds safe limits, a high-pitched alert will trigger security procedures that include

detaining the driver, using handheld equipment to identify
the type of radiation and notifying U.S. Customs and other
Federal safety officials. As giant cranes gingerly lift
containers on or off ships, the Coast Guard often keeps
watch with machine gun-tipped boats.[25]

A series of security enhancements are being put in
place by VPA, including the addition of video-surveillance
equipment, electronic fencing, biometrics-based
identification cards, high-tech lighting equipment and
additional police officers. Then there are the RIIDs: plans
call for installing 25 of the devices at VPA facilities. Bombs
are not the only threat. Weapons of mass destruction, such
as dry anthrax, could be easily shipped inside the huge
merchandise containers, or even snuck into a container
that sits at the dock for several days. New security
technology is a key component, but it's not a panacea.
VPA had planned to install powerful radiation sensors on
each of its 20 container cranes, which remove cargo from
vessels and place it on the docks for loading onto over-the-
road freight haulers. These devices, used to sniff out
radiation within containers and even identify potential
sources, had to be scrapped when Beta tests turned up
unreliable readings. Another high-powered technology that
uses Gamma rays was put on hold because of its cost.
These mobile portals (drive through portals) at $1 million a
piece, much more powerful than RIID, combine X-ray and
Geiger sensors, similar to that found on airport screening
devices. They are powerful enough to spot anomalies within
containers, including humans hiding inside.[26]

The port has issued new colour-coded identification
badges for employees and others who use the port, such
as shippers or suppliers. Each of the colours correspond to
a specific security level, and an alarm is sounded if a user

tries to use the card to gain access to unauthorized areas. Aware that cards can be counterfeited, however, VPA this year will embed the cards with biometric sensors, which scan physiological characteristics of users and match them against information in security databases.[27]

Global chain of custody

U.S. wants to introduce a global "chain of custody" for the world's 15 million shipping containers, so someone somewhere can always be held responsible for their contents. Such large scale initiatives warrant mammoth funding . Earlier, the likelihood of terrorist strikes on port was considered remote, if not unreal. hence the initial calls for big time spending were brushed off by authorities as unnecessary and 'serious money' was to be 'isolated from unwanted speculation'. However, in due course, federal funding was initiated along with serious measures in collaboration with other maritime states.

In 1999, the *Presidential Seaport Commission estimated each port would need to spend $44 million to provide state-of-the-art security.* In 2001, the American Association of Port Authorities went on record opposing a revised version of the reform bill.[28] 9/11 of course, ushered in a sea change. Federal grants began, helping offset some of the cost: for example in the above case, VPA received more than $5 million in grants from the Transportation Security Agency in 2002 , the third-highest amount of any U.S. port. Another $13 million in grants was requested. Most of the earlier funding was to help conform to the Maritime Transportation Security Act of 2002, which required both public and private ports to develop comprehensive security plans.

By July'2002 major federal spending was being undertaken. Congress provided the funding for the grant programme that was administered by the Maritime Administration and the U.S. Coast Guard on behalf of the Transportation Security Administration. In an effort to enhance the security of ports and other facilities, Secretary Mineta announced the award of $92.3 million in grants to 51 ports located throughout the country. Port security grants totaling $78 million were to fund enhanced facility and operational security, such as facility access control, physical security, cargo security and passenger security. In addition, $5 million were to go toward security assessments to enable port and terminals to evaluate vulnerabilities and identify mitigation strategies for their facilities. Also $9.3 million will fund "proof-of-concept" projects, which will explore the use of new technology, such as electronic seals, vessel tracking, and electronic notification of vessel arrivals, to improve maritime security.[29]

The Department also established an interagency "Credentialing Direct Action Group" (CDAG), co-chaired by MARAD[30], to examine the feasibility and process for potentially conducting background checks and issuing an identification card for all transportation workers and other persons who require access to secure areas of transportation facilities. On the international level, MARAD is the lead agency representing the United States at the ILO, which is addressing the Seaman's Credentialing issue. A target was set to have a new international convention on verifiable Seaman's identification completed by June 03.[31]

Interagency Container Working Group, led by the Department of Transportation and U.S. Customs, developed recommendations to improve security of containers as they move through the intermodal transportation system. The

Department's Intelligent Transportation Systems Joint Programme Office augmented the group's efforts by its successful completion of a test of electronic seals, a new technology that enabled regulatory agencies to determine if a container had been tampered with.[32] Recommendations addressed by the Working Group included, improving the coordination of government and business efforts as they relate to container security; enhancing data collection; improving the physical security of containers; initiating activities on the international front; and considering all possible uses of advanced technologies to improve the profiling and inspection of containers.[33]

CSI (Customs Container Security Initiative)

The U.S. Customs Container Security Initiative (CSI), proposed by Commissioner Bonner in a January 17, 2002 speech given at the Center for Strategic and International Studies, was a large-scale project undertaken to secure the U.S. bound/outbound containers. Each year, more than 16 million containers arrive in the United States by ship, truck, and rail. In 2001, U.S. Customs processed more than 214,000 vessels and 5.7 million sea containers. CSI was undertaken to tackle dangers that might be introduced through such commercial traffic.

The CSI consists of four core elements. These are:

(1) Establishing security criteria to identify high-risk containers;

(2) pre-screening containers before they arrive at U.S. ports;

(3) Using technology to pre-screen high-risk containers; and

(4) developing and using smart and secure containers.

The fundamental objective of the CSI was described as to first engage the ports that send the highest volumes of

container traffic into the United States *(see Table)*, as well
as the governments in these locations, in a way that will
facilitate detection of potential problems at their earliest
possible opportunity. The CSI approach was described as
not something that must be restricted to only these locations;
risk assessments and trade analysis would play an important
part in future deployments, it was said, and increased
security measures were described as vital to the operations
of any port in today's environment.[34]

A critical element in the success of this programme
was identified as the availability of advance information to
perform sophisticated targeting. The Port and Maritime
Security Act requires shippers to provide accurate manifest
information to the Customs Service before a ship arrives in
the United States. Commissioner Bonner now wanted the
information even before the cargo is loaded on the vessel.[35]

U.S. Customs then began to employ a multi-layered
strategy of targeting to sort out suspicious goods from
legitimate trade. The strategy relied heavily on the use of
strategic and tactical Intelligence to target incoming goods
for scrutiny. U.S. Customs pre-screened people and goods
entering the country at all 301 ports of entry. This long-
established screening process enabled U.S. Customs to
determine which containers may be — high-risk—and
which ones were nct. The goal of the CSI was to pre-
screen cargo containers at ports of origin or transit rather
than waiting for these goods to arrive in U.S. ports for
inspection.[36]

While the pre-screening that would be performed in
the CSI presented clear benefits to U.S. security, early
targeting of high-risk containers was cited to be potentially
of great value to the ports that had implemented heightened

security initiatives. A more secure maritime trade infrastructure would help ensure the continued smooth flow of merchandise through seaports. Ports that had implemented increased security and pre-screening become more attractive locations to those companies that depended on timely movement of merchandise or processing inputs. In the event of a catastrophic event involving the use of seagoing containers and subsequent paralysis of maritime trade, those ports that had participated in the CSI were to be well positioned to resume operations quickly and with the confidence of the trade community. In addition to these benefits, containers that do not present identifiable risks would, under normal circumstances, clear Customs rapidly, taking full advantage of the facilitative mechanisms that U.S. Customs had claimed to already been employing for some time.[37]

Mega-ports:

Flow of Container Traffic into the United States
Largest Foreign Ports of Departure

1. Hong Kong, China
2. Shanghai, China
3. Singapore
4. Kaohsiung, Taiwan
5. Rotterdam, Netherlands
6. Pusan, South Korea
7. Bremerhaven, Germany
8. Tokyo, Japan
9. Genoa, Italy
10. Yantian, China

Largest U.S. Ports of Import
1. NewYork
2. Los Angeles
3. Long Beach
4. Charleston
5. Seattle
6. Norfolk
7. Houston
8. Oakland
9. Savannah
10. Miami

Source: Journal of Commerce, January - October 2001.

The top 20 ports account for 68 percent of all cargo containers arriving at U.S. seaports. Governments representing 19 of these ports have agreed to implement CSI during the first phase including an agreement with the Government of Thailand for the Port of Laem Chabang that was signed by Secretary Ridge and Thailand's Foreign Minister on June 11, 2003. U.S. Secretary of Homeland Security, Tom Ridge, during an event at Port Elizabeth, New Jersey, highlighting the Department's efforts to secure U.S ports announced new port security initiatives and investments to provide increased International co-operation, greater use of technology and additional funds for port security facility enhancements.

Secretary Ridge claimed that the port security measures undertaken - both in the U.S. and abroad - are about building on capabilities and strengthening each layer of defence. Through information sharing with the international partners; several different levels of inspection; review of

Intelligence information on the crew cargo and vessel long before they reach the shores; state-of-the-art technology; and of course vigilance at every turn they are able to screen and board 100 percent of high-risk vessels coming into ports. The measures announced further build on a comprehensive port security strategy and range of enhancements directed by the President following September 11 2001. The announcements outlined below include the second phase of the Container Security Initiative (CSI), $170 million in port security grants and $58 million in funding for Operation Safe Commerce.[38]

These are some of the latest measures outlined by the Transport Security Administration, and announced by the Press Secretary, Department of Homeland Security.

Enhancing Container Security - Phase 2

The Container Security Initiative, an existing Department of Homeland Security programme which incorporates teamwork with foreign port authorities to identify target and search high-risk cargo, has now been expanded to strategic locations beyond the initial 20 major ports. this now includes areas of the Middle East such as Dubai as well as Turkey and Malaysia.

Secretary Ridge said, "Now that we have almost achieved our goal for CSI at nearly all of the top 20 ports, we will be expanding CSI to other ports that ship substantial amounts of cargo to the United States and that have the infrastructure and technology in place to participate in the programme." The top 20 ports account for 68 percent of all cargo containers arriving at U.S. seaports. Governments representing 19 of these ports have agreed to implement CSI during the first phase. Phase 2 of CSI will enable the Department to extend port security protection from 68

percent of container traffic to more than 80 percent—
casting the safety net of CSI far and wide.

Port Security Grants Programmes

Secretary Ridge announced a grant of $170 million dollars
for port security. The Port Security Grant Programme funds
security planning and projects to improve dockside and
perimeter security. The latest round of Transportation
Security Administration (TSA) grants have been awarded to
199 state and local governments and private companies for
$170 million. These new awards will contribute to important
security upgrades like new patrol boats in the harbour,
surveillance equipment at roads and bridges and the
construction of new command and control facilities. TSA,
United States Coast Guard and the Department of
Transportation's Maritime Administration evaluated the port
security grant applications and selected grant award
recipients. In 2002, $92 million was awarded in the first
round of port security grants.

In addition to the $170 million, the Department of
Homeland Security also provided $75 million in port
security grants for specific projects from the FY '03
supplemental budget. The funds will be distributed by the
Office for Domestic Preparedness to cover recent
infrastructure security protective measures, security
enhancement training exercises, equipment, planning and
information sharing.

Using Technology and Teamwork - Operation Safe Commerce

As part of the Department's effort to secure cargo as it
moves through the port, Secretary Ridge announced $58
million in funding for Operation Safe Commerce a pilot

programme in co-ordination with the Department of Transportation. This brings together private business, ports local state and federal representatives to analyze current security procedures for cargo entering the country. The programme's objective is to prompt research and development for emerging technology to monitor the movement and ensure the security and integrity of containers through the supply chain.

The ports of Seattle and Tacoma, Los Angeles and Long Beach and the Port Authority of New York/New Jersey are participating in the pilot programme.

To be totally secure, the whole maritime industry will have to undergo a radical overhaul. Thus the U.S. recognised the need to collaborate and rope in other administrations for ensuring maximum possible security. The awareness around the world is increasing and states likely to be targets for terror strikes have started considering serious security measures and thus echoing the sentiments that the campaigners of reform had been voicing well in advance.

Setting the Stage

Busy clusters on the maritime activity map have been voicing their concerns now and then. National agencies like The British National Union of Marine Aviation and Shipping Transport Officers called on the government to tighten the port regulations. They pointed out that on almost every level, the system is open to abuse. It was recommended that increasing use of seal experts, or preventive technology such as x-ray, gamma ray or vapour analysis to scan containers may help prevent the above stated threats.

However, such measures may add expenses that shippers are reluctant to incur. *Shipping companies would prefer to see government meet these added costs via general taxation*, as the ultimate benefit is greater public security.[39]

In December 2001, Singapore authorities arrested 15 suspected Islamist militants, with links to the Al Qaida, planning to blow up US naval vessels and a bus that was to transport American military service personnel.[40] A tape released by the Singapore government features a man describing how explosives could be carried on a bicycle without arousing suspicion. One plot involved bombing US Navy vessels in a special "kill zone" along the northeastern shores of Singapore and the bus that was targeted carried US military personnel between a naval base used by visiting warships and a train station. The US Navy has a logistics unit in Singapore, and warships going to and from Afghanistan have been docked for replenishment in the new naval facility specially designed to accommodate US aircraft carriers.

Thus, major maritime hubs have been decidedly more vigilant and further co-operation has been solicited by US authorities. Different departments of maritime commerce and agencies with varied business interests are now seeking to work together towards achieving a more secure marine environment. Law enforcement and Industry must interface so that they understand the basics of good marine loss control, and as a result industry professionals, such as surveyors and maritime security personnel, can show the police how the mechanics of the industry work and how knowledge of the industry helps the educated perpetrator cover his crimes.

The maritime industry and marine insurance industry are starting to share loss data with each other as well as law enforcement. Examples include: American Institute of

Marine Underwriters large loss reporting system etc, and forums are developing for the exchange of information such as the National Cargo Security Council etc.[41]

The stage is set therefore, for National/Regional/ International Action from governments, identification of common concerns. Co-operative actions through bilateral, multilateral actions and/or International Conventions on issues where appropriate is now in hand.

First International Act :The Focus of the ISPS Code on Port Facilities

A new, comprehensive security regime for International shipping is set to enter into force in July 2004 following the adoption by a week-long Diplomatic Conference of a series of measures to strengthen maritime security and prevent and suppress acts of terrorism against shipping. The Conference, held at the London Headquarters of the International Maritime Organization (IMO) from 9 to 13 December, was of crucial significance not only to the International Maritime Community but the World Community as a whole, given the pivotal role shipping plays in the conduct of world trade. The measures represent the culmination of just over a year's intense work by IMO's Maritime Safety Committee and its Intercessional Working Group since the terrorist atrocities in the United States in September 2001.

The Conference was attended by 108 contracting governments to the 1974 SOLAS Convention, observers from two IMO Member States and observers from the two IMO Associate Members. United Nations specialized agencies, intergovernmental organizations and non-governmental international organizations also sent observers to the Conference.

The Conference adopted a number of amendments to the 1974 Safety of Life at Sea Convention (SOLAS), the most far-reaching of which enshrines the new International Ship and Port Facility Security Code (ISPS Code). The code contains detailed security-related requirements for governments, port authorities and shipping companies in a mandatory section (Part A), together with a series of guidelines about how to meet these requirements in a second, non-mandatory section (Part B). The Conference also adopted a series of resolutions designed to add weight to the amendments, encourage the application of the measures to ships and port facilities not covered by the code and pave the way for future work on the subject.[42]

The objective of the ISPS code is to establish an International framework involving co-operation between contracting governments, government agencies, local administration and the shipping and port industries to detect/assess security threats and take preventive measures against security incidents affecting ships and port facilities used in International trade; to establish the roles and responsibilities of all these parties concerned, at the national and international level, for:

1) ensuring maritime security, 2) to ensure early and sufficient collation and exchange of security related information 3) to provide a methodology for security assessments so as to have plans and procedures to react to changing security levels and 4) to ensure confidence that adequate and proportionate maritime security measures are in place. These objectives are achieved by 5) designation of appropriate officers/personnel in each ship, in each port facility and each shipping company. 6) to prepare and put into effect the security plans that'll be approved for each ship and port facility.

Thus   based upon the above principles, in a broad overview, the mandatory Part A of the ISPS Code has the following sections dealing with port facility security:

Section 14- Port Facility Security.

Section 15- Port Facility Security Assessment (PFSA).

Section 16- Port Facility Security Plan (PFSP).

Section 17- Port Facility Security Officer (PFSO).

Section 18- Training, drills and exercises on Port Facility Security.

Part B which provides guidance on compliance with Part A of the Code also has 2 appendices:

Appendix I - Form of a Declaration of Security between a Ship and a Port Facility.

Appendix II - Form of a Statement of Compliance of a Port Facility.

The new Chapter XI-2 of SOLAS 74 as amended, "Special measures to enhance maritime security", defines a port facility as a location, as determined by the contracting government (to the SOLAS Convention) or by the Designated Authority, where the ship/port interface takes place. This includes areas such as anchorages, waiting berths and approaches from seawards, as appropriate.

It further asserts that this chapter (and hence the code) applies to:

The following types of ships engaged on international voyages: passenger ships including high-speed passenger craft - and cargo ships, including high speed craft, of 500 gross tonnage and upwards; and

Port facilities serving such ships engaged on International voyages.

It, however, states that the contracting governments shall decide the extent of application of this chapter on port facilities within their territories. (Regulation 2)

Regulation XI-2/6 covers requirements for port facilities, providing among other things for Contracting Governments to ensure that port facility security assessments are carried out and that port facility security plans are developed, implemented and reviewed in accordance with the ISPS Code.

The Port Facility- ISPS Perspective

Each contracting government has to ensure completion of a Port Facility Security Assessment for each port facility within its territory that serves ships engaged on International voyages. The Port Facility Security Assessment is fundamentally a risk analysis of all aspects of a port facility's operation in order to determine which parts of it are more susceptible, and/or more likely, to be the subject of attack.. Security assessments will have three essential components. First, they must identify and evaluate important assets and infrastructures that are critical to the port facility as well as those areas or structures that, if damaged, could cause significant loss of life or damage to the port facility's economy or environment. Secondly, the assessment must identify the actual threats to those critical assets and infrastructure in order to prioritize security measures. Finally, the assessment must address vulnerability of the port facility by identifying its weaknesses in physical security, structural integrity, protection systems, procedural policies, communication systems, transportation infrastructure, utilities, and other areas within a port facility that may be a likely target. Once this assessment has been completed, contracting Government can accurately evaluate risk.

Security risk is seen as a function of the threat of an attack coupled with the vulnerability of the target and the consequences of an attack. In order to communicate the threat at a port facility or for a ship, the Contracting Government will set the appropriate security level. Security levels 1, 2, and 3 correspond to normal, medium, and high threat situations, respectively. The security level creates a link between the ship and the port facility, since it triggers the implementation of appropriate security measures for the ship and for the port facility.

On completion of the analysis, it will be possible to produce an overall assessment of the level of risk. The port facility security assessment will help determine which port facilities are required to appoint a port facility security officer and prepare a port facility security plan. This plan should indicate the operational and physical security measures the port facility should take to ensure that it always operates at security level 1. The plan should also indicate the additional, or intensified, security measures the port facility can take to move to and operate at security level 2 when instructed to do so. It should also indicate the possible preparatory actions the port facility could take to allow prompt response to the instructions that may be issued at security level3.

Ships using port facilities may be subject to port state control inspections and additional control measures. The relevant authorities may request the provision of information regarding the ship, its cargo, passengers and ship's personnel prior to the ship's entry into port. There may be circumstances in which entry into port could be denied.

This risk management concept wiil be embodied in the Code through a number of minimum functional security requirements for ships and port facilities.

For port facilities, the requirements will include:

- port facility security plans.
- port facility security officers.
- certain security equipment.

In addition the requirements for ships and for port facilities include:

- monitoring and controlling access.
- monitoring the activities of people and cargo.
- ensuring security communications are readily available etc.

Prevention—not the Cure Yet

Section 5 of the Preamble of the ISPS Code mentions that the extension of SOLAS-74 to cover port facilities was agreed on the basis that SOLAS-74 offered the speediest means of ensuring the necessary security measures entered into force and given effect quickly. However, it was further agreed, that the provisions relating to the port facilities should relate solely to ship/port interface. The wider issue of the security of port areas will be the subject of further joint work between the International Maritime Organisation and the International Labour Organisation. It was also agreed that the provisions should not extend to the actual response to attacks or to any necessary clear up activities after such an attack.

Thus, the ISPS Code has set the pace for measures to be taken on an international level, it is not as yet a comprehensive manual for all security initiatives needed to be undertaken to ensure a totally secure port. Thus, a holistic, informed , responsive to a dynamic and changing security environment setup is essential and as such these adjectives should be applicable to all levels of the sector and not just to the administration.

Conclusion

The Fifth Horseman's 'gift' landing on a port today is an event not in the realms of fiction anymore.

Ports are the real pressure points on the commerce lifelines. They are the nations openings to the outside world and thus the most likely source of toxins seeping into the intermodal transport network. If cleverly executed and masterminded - a weapon can reach up to any strategic location in a country - originating from the open nerve ending of a port.

Effect a port and a country's whole economical circulation can come to a standstill.

A uniform response is thus necessitated not just locally, but from around the globe. The leading maritime nations have identified the threat imposed and have begun to take initiatives. The whole maritime industry needs to respond as an inter-knitted network with a common goal: to protect the worlds ports and shipping traffic from all kinds of hostile activity.

Loopholes in the system need to be specifically targeted. There is a need to champion the cause of more transparent systems and appreciate the value of a safe and secure environment. Nation states have to establish security systems for their ports and fleets. Funds have to be raised if required so by general taxation or by grants. Agencies like the Coast Guard, Customs, Navies etc. should be well funded, organised and prepared. In establishing a security oriented regime, it is imperative that all players , including private individuals and enterprises are covered and a system of awareness, conformity and review established.

Measures taken have to be in step with the latest trends in technological innovations; and increasing use of Intelligence gathering and exchange is to be made.

The scene is set for Regional/National/ International and multilateral co-operation. The advent of the ISPS code and its entering into force on July '04 will demand compliance with minimum security standards from the contracting governments. But there is no all encompassing definition of a perfect security measure. With a complex variety of intrusion possibilities from the sea, (the possibilities themselves increasing as new means become available), the security setup will have to be evolving all the time, keeping in step as well as incorporating all the latest on the tactical and technological scene.

The immediate need is, therefore, to establish the platform for a security setup, an evolutionary model dynamically responding to newer challenges.

Scientific growth and accompanying innovations establish a more secure environment than the one prevalent prior to its installation. However, these systems bring about their own new vulnerabilities and susceptibilities demanding an organisation dealing with it to be up to date and just not complacent. Such technological growth related new susceptibilities and 'viruses' hitherto unseen can only be tackled by agencies which are based on the foundations of efficient Intelligence gathering and awareness, technical suaveness, quick and effective responsiveness, preparedness for all contingencies, cooperativeness and have at their disposal funds, resources and multilateral assistance to carry out their task.

The agencies should ensure a well protected port and that potential risks should be eliminated well outside the perimeter of the port.

Port Security: India

To reiterate what marine security analysts have been voicing since a long time – all security measures should start by securing the nations receptors to the outside world-its ports. In India we have a total of 12 major Ports. To instil state of the Art Security equipment in these would entail an expenditure of almost 44 millions dollars per port or 528 million dollar overall for the major ports. This is a mammoth sum and we will have to prioritise the expenditure and proceed in stages.

Notes

1. "War on Terrorism", Paul Harris and Martin Bright *The Observer* Sunday December 23, 2001.
2. ICC's Commercial Crime Service Report of London, 20th Dec'2002.
3. From: ERRI DAILY INTELLIGENCE REPORT 01 Dec 2001 see http://www.emergency.com/hzmtpage.htm.
4. "Port of Entry Now Means Point of Anxiety", *The New York Times*, December 23, 2001.
5. " U.S. Ports Represent Weakness in Nation's Defenses, Analysis Shows", Knight Ridder/Tribune, October 30, 2001
6. *Ibid.*
7. Martin Bright, Paul Harrisand and Nick Paton Walsh The Observer Sunday December 23, 2001
8. *Ibid.*
9. From: ERRI DAILY INTELLIGENCE REPORT-Monday, December 24, 2001-Christmas Eve-Vol. 7 – 360
10. From: ERRI DAILY INTELLIGENCE REPORT 02 Mar2002 see http://www.emergency.com/hzmtpage.htm
11. Virginia Business, May 2003, Gary Kranz
12. *The New York Times*, December 12, 2002
13. From: ERRI DAILY INTELLIGENCE REPORT 01 Dec 2001 see http://www.emergency.com/hzmtpage.htm
14. " U.S. Ports Represent Weakness in Nation's Defenses, Analysis Shows", *Knight Ridder/Tribune*, October 30, 2001

15. "Port security tightens", Gary Kranz Virginia business, May 2003,

16. *Ibid.*

17. *Ibid.*

18. From: ERRI DAILY INTELLIGENCE REPORT 01 Dec 2001 see http://www.emergency.com/hzmtpage.htm

19. Virginia Business, May 2003, Gary Kranz

20. *Knight Ridder/Tribune*, October 30, 2001

21. Virginia Business, May 2003, Gary Kranz

22. *Knight Ridder/Tribune*, October 30, 2001

23. *Ibid.*

24. Virginia Business, May 2003, Gary Kranz

25. *Ibid.*

26. *Ibid.*

27. *Ibid.*

28. *Knight Ridder/Tribune*, October 30, 2001

29. Remarks by Maritime Administrator Captain William G. Schubert, Navy League National Convention — Sea Service Panel Marriott Marquis Hotel – New York, NY, July 2, 2002

30. MARAD stands for Maritime Administration of the U.S.

31. Remarks by Maritime Administrator Captain William G. Schubert, Navy League National Convention — Sea Service Panel Marriott Marquis Hotel – New York, NY, July 2, 2002

32. The in-transit (SMART CONTAINER) cargo security system accurately records information prior to, and immediately after an unauthorized intrusion incident which will provide surveyors and claims adjustors incident time, date, and location information that is currently not easily determined.

33. Captain William G. Schubert, Navy League National Convention, New York, NY, July 2, 2002.

34. *U.S. Customs Today*, March' 2002, also see fact sheet on CSI ,Feb'2002 distributed by the Office of International Information Programmes, U.S. Department of State. (Web site: http://usinfo.state.gov)

35. *Ibid.*

36. *Ibid.*

37. *Ibid.*

38. Press releases, "Secretary Ridge Announces New Initiatives For Port Security", Office of the Press Secretary, U.S.. DEPARTMENT OF HOMELAND SECURITY June 12, 2003

39. ICC's Commercial Crime Service Report of London, 20th Dec'2002

40. "Singapore Says Terror Ring Planned Attacks on Americans", *Los Angeles Times,* January 12, 2002. The terror cell, which called itself Jemaah Islamiah, had been reportedly operating in Singapore for years and many of its cadres had traveled to Afghanistan for weapons training in camps run by Osama Bin Laden's Al Qaida network. Singapore Defense Minister Tony Tan said that the terrorists had planned to blow up embassies and military installations. *Also see* http://www.pakistanlink.com/headlines/Jan/08/07.html

41. John M. Tichenor , Cigna Marine Services

42. See : http://www.imo.org

‹5›

Terrorist Equipment Profiles

General
The aim of this chapter is to briefly acquaint Merchant Navy officers and sailors as also laymen with the typology of equipment currently being employed by terrorist groups. Familiarity with the weapons and equipment being employed can assist in early detection and quick reading\accurate reporting of incidents of terrorist attacks\piracy on sea.

Small Arms
AK-47 Kalashnikov Rifle (Automatic Kalashnikov-Obrazets 1947g)

The legendary Kalashnikov (AK-47) rifle has become the prime liet motif of terror all over the globe. This was designed in the Soviet Union by the legendary designer Mikhail Timoteyevich Kalashnikov at the end of World War II and has since then become one of the most extensively produced and employed weapon systems in the world (over 50 million were produced). It is a simple, robust and handy weapon of good design and excellent workmanship. Professionals call it "jam proof and idiot proof." The Chinese NORINCO industries have also mass produced copies of this 7.62mm assault rifle. This Chinese version is called Type 56. The Chinese model can be identified by the Chinese characters on the right hand side of the receiver. A number of East European countries as well as Egypt also produce versions of this rifle under license. Terrorists use AKs from all sources. The CIA had purchased these in bulk from China and Egypt and provided them to the Mujahideen in Afghanistan through Pakistan's Inter Services Intelligence (ISI). From Afghanistan these have travelled to various terrorist outfits. Pakistan's ISI has also directly provided AK series of rifles to terrorists in J&K, Bosnia, Chechenya, Tajikistan and Uzbekistan (as also in Xinjiang province of China). Soviet model AKs were also captured in Afghanistan by the Mujahideen and these are also available ex Darra Adam Khels arms Bazaar of the North West Frontier Province in Pakistan to the terrorists. Another source of illegal weapons in recent times has been Cambodia (through the Khemer Rouge insurgents) and the various rebel groups in Myanmar. There are several versions of the AK. The standard versions have a wooden shoulder stock. However, the Chinese 56c model has plastic replacing the wooden components. The Type 56.2 have a butt stock which folds sideways. Characteristic feature of the AK series is it's long curved magazine.

Salient Characteristics

(a) Bore—7.62mm

(b) Operation—gas, selective fire

(c) Feed-30 rounds detachable magazine(curved shape)

(d) Weight—3.8 kg

(e) Length—874mm.645mm.Stock Folded(56-112)

(f) Maximum Effective Range—400 meters

The standard rifles in world armies till the 1960s were 7.62mm bore weapons. The current trend is towards standardization around the 5.56mm bore and even smaller bores(5.45mm).The aim is to make the weapons lighter and smaller and have weapons that wound in preference to killing. Accordingly, Russian built AK-74 is a much smaller version of this weapon in the 5.45mm bore and is generally used by paratroopers. It is also a favourite weapon of terrorists due to it's smaller size which offers better chances of concealment under clothes etc.

The Heckler Koch G3 Rifle

Another 7.62mm assault rifle that is encountered with terrorists is the 7.62mm German Heckler and Koch G3 rifle. It is the standard rifle of the German and Pakistani armies. A number of terrorist outfits in South and South East Asia are equipped with this standard assault rifle. It can be distinguished from the AK-47 by it's smaller and straighthedged magazine and relatively much longer foregraurd. It was also used by the erstwhile Somali army and hence may well be encountered with terrorists pirates off the coast of Africa.

Salient Characteristics

(a) Bore—7.62mm

(b) Feed—20 round magazine

(c) Weight—4.4 kg

(d) Length—1025mm.with retracted butt 840mm

(e) Maximum Effective Range—400m.

Dragunov Sniper Rifle (Ots-03 AS)SVU

This is a deadly sniper rifle of Russian origin. It has a smaller 10 round box magazine and has a telescopic sight. It's maximum effective range is 800 to 1000m. It has a very high powered bullet that can penetrate a steel helmet at 1800m. Chinese versions of this sniper rifle manufactured by NORINCO are also available. This sniper rifle can be used to hit lookout personnel on ship or eliminate key personnel in critical areas. It is also manufactured by Iran and Romania.

Pistols

The pistols most likely to be encountered with terrorist groups are the Chinese (NORINCO)7.62mm Madine Pistol Type 80.This was based on the German Mauser design. It has now been replaced by the NORINCO 9mm Type59 pistol which is a copy of the Russian Makarov pistol. This has an eight round magazine and has empty weight of 730gms.The 9mm bore is now the standard bore for pistols in most of the world's armies.

RPG-7 Rocket Launchers

Another standard equipment in the terrorist armoury is the RPG Russian Anti Tank Rocket Launcher. This is a very light weight and versatile rocket launcher and remains the standard man portable, short range anti-tank weapon in the Russian, East European,Chinese,Pakistani and Indian armies. The RPG-7 is similar to the earlier RPG-2 and both have a bore diameter of 40mm.The RPG-2, however, is straight and tubular while the RPG-7 has a bell shaped mouth at the rear for the escape of the blast gases. The RPG-7 fires the PG-7 and PG-7m anti-tank grenade(73mm diameter)which has a HEAT(High Explosive Anti Tank) or shaped warhead that can penetrate 400mm of armour plating. This is a standard weapon used by terrorists for ambushing and destroying vehicles and has been used against ships in the Somali coast by terrorists\pirates.

Salient Characteristics

(a) Caliber—40mm

(b) Length of Launcher—950mm

(c) Weight—6.3kg

(d) Range-
     Moving—350m
     Static—500m

(e) Armour Penetration—400mm

Hand grenades

photo courtesy: US department of defense

Broadly speaking, a grenade is just a small bomb designed for short-range use.The essential elements of a grenade, then, are combustible material and an ignition system. Ignition systems also vary, but they generally fall into one of two categories: time-delay igniters and impact igniters. The function of both systems is to set off the explosion after the grenade is a good distance away from the thrower. The igniter in an impact grenade is activated by the force of the grenade landing on the ground. With a time-delay grenade, the thrower sets off a fuze, a mechanism that ignites the grenade after a certain amount of time has passed (generally a few seconds).

The most common type of grenade on the battlefield is the time-delay fragmentation anti-personnel hand grenade. The primary function of this grenade is to kill or maim nearby enemy troops. To ensure maximum damage, the grenade is designed to launch dozens of small metal fragments in every direction when it explodes.

These sorts of grenades, which played a major role in World War I, World War II, Vietnam and many other 20th century conflicts, are designed to be durable, easy to use and easy to manufacture. The conventional design uses a simple chemical delay mechanism. The diagram below shows a typical configuration of this system, dating back to the first World War. The outer shell of the grenade, made of serrated cast iron, holds a chemical fuze mechanism, which is surrounded by a reservoir of explosive material. The grenade has a filling hole for pouring in the explosive material.

Usage method: Depress the striker lever, pull the pin, hurl the grenade.

Explosives

RDX and PEK are some of the standard explosives that are used by the terrorists. Specially trained sniffer dogs can help to detect these. PEK looks like yellow plastercene and can be tamped into any shape for making charges. Normal dynamite/gelatin sticks used for basting in mines or road construction are also used. Improvised Explosive Devices

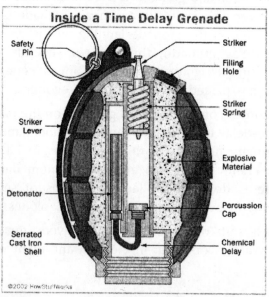

Inside a Time Delay Grenade

Safety Pin
Striker
Filling Hole
Striker Spring
Striker Lever
Explosive Material
Detonator
Percussion Cap
Serrated Cast Iron Shell
Chemical Delay

©2002 HowStuffWorks

(IED) are made from any of the above and can be activated remotely by using hand held radio sets from a distance of 2-300 meters or more.

Plastic Explosives

The basic idea of plastic explosives, also called plastic bonded explosives (PBX), is to combine explosive chemicals with a plastic binder material. The binder serves two purposes:

* It coats the explosive material, so it's less sensitive to shock and heat. This makes it relatively safe to handle the explosive.
* It makes the explosive material highly malleable. You can mold it into different shapes to change the direction of the explosion

Plastic explosives such as pentaerythritol tetranitrate (PETN) and hexahydro-1,3,5-triazine (RDX for "research development explosive") pose serious threats because (1) they are easily to mold into desired shapes, (2) they remain highly stable until detonated, and (3) they can inflict significant damage even in small amounts.

A candidate for "the first plastic explosive" would be the original blasting gelatins manufactured by Nobel himself. These were mixtures of nitroglycerine and nitrocellulose. A practical plastic explosive based on TNT was patented 1905.

Plastic explosives have been in use since World War II and in the 1960s found their way into the malevolent hands of terrorists. Two of the most extensively used explosives are outlined below, these have been used with devastating effects all around the world.

*A chunk of Cordex, a military brand of plastic explosives. Highly
stable, very destructive. Includes a timer, which is ticking.*

C-4

C-4, an advanced plastic explosive, was used in the
attack on the USS Cole, according to Yemen's prime minister
and sources close to the U.S. investigation. Seventeen U.S.
sailors were killed and 39 others wounded when a small
boat loaded with explosives pulled up next to the Cole
while it was docked for refueling and exploded. The
explosion tore a 40-by-40 foot hole in the side of the
destroyer. Investigators say the bombers launched their small
boat six miles from where the Cole was refueling. The trip
across the harbor would have taken 20 minutes. Shortly
after the attack, bomb-making materials were found in an
apartment near the harbor.

C-4 is a commercial grade explosive that appears similar
to putty or clay and requires a blasting cap to ignite.

The explosive material in C-4 is RDX. The additive
material is made up of polyisobutylene, the binder, and
di(2-ethylhexyl) sebacate, the plasticizer (the element that
makes the material malleable). It also contains a small
amount of motor oil and some 2, 3-dimethyl-2, 3-
dinitrobutane (DMDNB), which functions as a chemical
marker for security forces. The result is a relatively stable,
solid explosive with a consistency similar to modelling clay.
A detonator or a blasting cap is used to ignite the explosive,
detonator being a relatively easy explosive to set off such

as an electric charge; these detonators can also be remotely controlled.

Less than a pound of C-4 could potentially kill several people, to take out one 8-inch (20.3-centimeter) square steel beam, for example, one would probably use 8 to 10 pounds (3.6 to 4.5 kilograms) of C-4. Indonesian investigators have recovered traces of C-4 plastic explosives at the scene of the bombing in Bali that killed at least 181 people. Because of its stability and sheer destructive power, C-4 has attracted the attention of terrorists and guerilla fighters all over the world. A small amount of C-4 can do a lot of damage, and it's fairly easy to smuggle the explosive past light security measures. The U.S. military is the primary manufacturer of C-4, and it tightly guards its supply, but there are a number of other sources for similar explosive material (including Iran, which has a history of conflict with the United States). As long as it is readily accessible, C-4 will continue to be a primary weapon in the terrorist arsenal.

Semtex

Stanislav Brebera spent much of his life developing Semtex, the best plastic explosive in the world. It feels like Play Dough, has no smell, and was designed in 1966 to clear land-mines and improve industrial safety. It is also undetectable by dogs and airport security devices, and after it left Mr. Brebera's laboratory in 1968, Semtex became the favored weapon of international terrorists from Libya to Northern Ireland. Named after Semtin, the village in East Bohemia where Brebera invented it, this extraordinarily stable compound of RDX (Cyclonite) and PETN (Penaerythrite Tetranitrate) slips through airport security scans as easily as a pair of nylons. According to the FBI, Semtex has an indefinite shelf life and is far stronger than traditional explosives such as TNT. It is also easily available on the black market.

Like its American-made counterpart C-4, Semtex in and of itself is relatively harmless and can be easily handled. A blasting cap or piece of detonating cord is required to set it off. The two main components of Semtex, RDX (Cyclonite) and PETN (Pentaerythrite Tetranitrate), both powerful explosives in their own right, can be produced cheaply by someone with the right chemical know-how and a simple laboratory. Sources close to U.S. intelligence agencies say that tons of the explosive were funneled through Libya by the former Soviet Union and other Eastern Bloc nations back in the 1970s and '80s. From there, the Libyan government is believed to have distributed Semtex to the Irish Republican Army and Iraq, along with various miliant groups in the Middle East, according to military analysts at Jane's Information Group. The IRA is said to possess 3 metric tons of Semtex, according to Jane's.

Semtex became infamous when just 12 ounces of the substance, molded inside a Toshiba cassette recorder, blasted Pan Am flight 103 out of the sky above Lockerbie, Scotland, in December 1988, killing 270 people. A year later, after the Czech Communist regime was toppled, the new president, Vaclav Havel, revealed that the Czechs had exported 900 tons of Semtex to Col. Moammar Qaddafi's Libya and another 1,000 tons to other unstable states, such as Syria, North Korea, Iraq, and Iran. Some experts now put worldwide stockpiles of Semtex at 40,000 tons.

Plastic explosives can be smuggled in virtually any inventable form and terrorists have managed to get in the explosive on board flights using pregnancy prosthetics, hiding the explosive in shoes and electronic gadgets etc.

The Convention on the Marking of Plastic Explosives for the Purpose of Detection requires States Parties to mark plastic explosives they manufacture with a chemical agent which can be detected by commercially available vapor/particle trace detectors and canines. There is a need to educate mariners and security strategists to be aware of the threat posed by plastic explosives while implementing security measures .

Radio Sets

Generally, the terrorists use hand held light weight radio sets that are commercially available eg.Kenwood,Yeasu and Motorolas.They make short transmissions and use localised code words or nick names to provide low grade cover. They also use radio sets to detonate IEDs.

Notes

1. Most weapon characteristics and photographs are from the authoritative "Janes Infantry Weapons".

‹6›

The Indian Context

The Indian Economic Scenario

According to World Bank Projections, India is likely to become the world's fourth largest economy (after China, USA and Japan) by the year 2020, in terms of Purchasing Power Parity (PPP). For the past decade the Indian economy has been growing at an average rate of between 5-6 percent. The country's Gross Domestic Product (GDP) real growth rate in 1992-97 in fact averaged at 6.9 percent. This included a peak of 7.8 percent in 1994-95 and 1996-97. The Indian economy's net worth in 1998-99 was 418.96 billion dollars.

It is noteworthy that the world GDP growth rates in 1998-99 were less than 3 percent. The Indian real growth of the GDP dipped in 1999-2000 but was still pegged at 5.9 percent or 448 billion dollars. It declined due to bad monsoons in 2001-02 and 2002-03 to 5.6 % and 4.4% respectively but was again pegged at 8% in 2003 (479 billion dollars). In 1998-99 India's foreign trade of 75.52 billion dollars (Rs 317,708 crore) accounted for 18.03% of GDP. This rose in 1999-2000 to 83.69 billion dollars and accounted for 18.68 percent of India's GDP. The Indian economy scaled new height in 2003-04 and the rate of growth of the GDP reached the 8 percent mark.

Maritime Trade

India has a coastline of 7600 kms. It has 12 major and 184 minor ports. Some 75 percent of India's foreign trade in Value and 97 percent in Volume is sea borne. In fact in the year 1998-99, as much as 56.64 billion dollars worth of goods and commodities (244.15 million tons) were handled at India's major ports. This averaged to a 155.18 million dollars worth and 668,904 tons per day.

Merchant Marine

In terms of mercantile marine India has a fleet strength of 510 ships with 7.05 million Gross Registered Tons (GRT) as on 01 Jan 2000. In 1999 India's shipping fleet constituted 1.27 percent of the worlds shipping tonnage (and ranked 17th in the worlds ship registries). India's shipping tonnage has been stagnating since 1996 (when it had reached 7 million GRT). Only 29.8 percent of India's foreign trade is carried on Indian ships (1996-97 figures). Approximately, 43 % of India's tonnage (3.04 million GRT) is carried in 118 ships. The rest is shared among 79 other shipping companies. It is hoped that India's mercantile fleet will grow in the coming years and take on the bulk of Indian overseas trade.

Energy Security

In India crude oil is the second largest commercial fuel (accounting for 27 percent of the share) after coal (61 percent) and followed by Natural Gas (9%), Hydroelectric Power (2%) and Nuclear Power (1%).

In 1997-98 imports of crude oil accounted for 50 percent of the demand and domestic offshore oil 33 percent. In effect 83% of the country's demand for crude oil was met by the maritime sector. In 1995 as many as 3810 oil tanker visits took place at Indian ports with 2295 visits on the West Coast and 1515 visits on the East Coast. These averaged to almost 10 visits per day. The Port wise visit profile on the West Coast was:

- Mumbai – 778 visits
- Kandla – 642
- Vadinan – 114

The East Coast Profile

- Haldia – 594
- Chennai – 462
- Vishakhpatnam – 371

Oil imports are rising exponentially

India is far more dependant than the USA or even Western Europe on the import of crude oil from West Asia. Up to 90 percent of India's oil imports were sourced from West Asia compared to 19 % for US and 74% for Japan. West Asia is critical not just for the oil but also is the epicenter of a rising tide of Muslim fundamentalism and Islamic angst.

The threats to Indian maritime trade, shipping, mercantile fleet and port Infrastructure is patent and obvious. Along with the USA and Israel, India is one of the prime targets for Islamic terrorist outfits. Pakistan's ISI has been funding a Muslim *Jehad* in Kashmir for well over a decade. Kashmir may be a land centric Low Intensity conflict. What is however the cause for serious concern is the attempt of Pakistans ISI to spread Jehadi terrorism to all parts of India. In March 1993 the ISI smuggled in huge quantities of explosives on to India's West Coast. These were used to stage massive bomb blasts in the Port city of Mumbai, which is the commercial capital of the country.

From 1987-1990 the Indian Armed Forces conducted major Peace Keeping Operations in Sri Lanka against the

LTTE – a major terrorist group which is now also involved in Narcotics smuggling and extensive gun running. Since the 1980s the LTTE has developed and operated an extensive fleet of 10-12 well maintained freighters flying Panamian, Honduran and Liberian flags. The majority of cargo is legitimate (e.g. hard wood, tea, coconuts, fertilisers etc). These earn revenue for LTTE. However, some 5 percent capacity is utilised for smuggling arms and ammunition. The Indian Navy has for a long time been engaged in operations to check LTTE smuggling of weapons and explosives along India's Southern Coast line. Post the 1993 bomb blasts in Mumbai such operations were also launched along the Western Coastline.

The Mumbai Bomb Blasts

Mumbai is the commercial capital of India and boasts of two massive ports. The Mumbai Port alone receives 778 visits by oil tankers every year. This massive commercial hub center and metropolis has been a favourite target of terrorists sponsored by Pakistan's infamous ISI. Most of the violent incidents staged in Mumbai have been carried out by the terrorist outfits employing the local mafia gangs. The first major terrorist incident in Mumbai occurred in March 1993. Doud Ibrahim and Tiger Memon, former Mumbai mafia dons who had based themselves in Dubai and later Karachi and had become one of the prime assets of the ISI, staged a series of 13 massive bomb blasts in Mumbai. These led to a staggering toll of over 300 people killed and 1330 injured. The large quantity of high explosives used in these blasts had been smuggled on to the West Coast of India using the traditional dhows and other smuggling conduits for contraband.

Mumbai has been plagued by a series of bomb blasts thereafter. There were blasts in Ghatkopar that killed 12 and left 75 injured. A fresh round of blasts started on 02 May 1999. Blasts in the suburban train in Victoria station killed 2 people and wounded 5. On 06 Dec 2002 there were two blasts that killed 7 people. On 27 June 2003 there was another blast at Vile Parle which killed 1 and left 25 wounded. On 13 Mar 2003 there was yet another blast in a train in Mumbai that left 11 dead and 65 injured. On 25 May 2003 there were two more bomb blasts in the crowded Veli and Zaveuri Bazaars near the Gateway of India that left 46 dead and over 150 injured. This was the 6th blast in the last nine months and shook up the security agencies. Most of these blasts had a communal agenda aimed at sparking off riots. The threat to India's major Port city is real and ominous. India's Ports thus are a major vulnerability. To instal state of the art security equipment in the 12 major ports would need an outlay of 528 million dollars. If the 182 odd minor Ports are also included, the expenditure involved would be 8.62 billion dollars. This gives us an idea of the magnitude of the task involved.

Operation Cactus

One of the most significant anti-terrorist operations was the Indian intervention in Maldives in Nov. 1988. This was code named **Operation Cactus.** This was the first instance of an island nation perse being almost taken over by a terrorist group. Information reached New Delhi that a large group of about 150 terrorists of the PLOTE Group led by Abdullah Luthufi had dis-embarked at Hulele ; the capital of the Maldives and staged an armed coup. They landed in two Trawlers. They had surrounded the Presidential Palace and the Presidential Guard had just managed to stave them off and hold out. The Maldives Government was under siege from terrorists. In a high voltage drama, India launched an air assault with a Para Battalion Group (based on 5 Para) led by Brigadier Balsara, the Commander of India's Para Brigade himself. It was a tricky operation. The huge IL-76 aircrafts managed to land at Hulele Air port after nightfall. The Paras quickly secured the Airfield, commandeered boats, fanned out and lifted the siege of the Presidential Palace and rescued President Gayoom. The terrorist group fled in a ship named *M.V Progress Light* on 3 November They took the Transport minister, his wife and several other citizens hostage. This ship was given chase by the Indian Navy and in another dramatic operation, it was tracked down and intercepted by two Indian Naval Ships, the *INS Godavri* and *Betwa*. The hostages were safely rescued by 6 Nov 1988.

India has the third largest military airlift capability after the USA and Russia and this paid handsome dividends in this rescue operation against a terrorist attempt to hijack a micro Island nation State itself.

Operation Leech

In the year 1998, the Indian Navy launched **Operation Leech** to apprehend a group of Thai and other terrorists trying to smuggle a huge haul of weapons. These were intercepted in the Andaman group of Islands after a dramatic chase and captured.

The Alondra Rainbow

The *MV Alondra Rainbow* was a 7000 ton Japanese Merchant Vessel. It was carrying tin ingots from Indonesia to Japan. An organised gang of pirates observed the vessel leaving the port and boarded the ship. They set the crew adrift in a boat. Thai fishermen later picked up 10 crew members 60 nautical miles off the West Coast of Satun.

The pirates had apparently negotiated a sale of the cargo. When the ship did not reach its destination port, the Piracy Center of the International Maritime Bureau at Kaulalumpur put out an International alert. A few days later the master of an Indian merchant vessel noticed a ship that resembled the *Alondra Rainbow*. Its name had been freshly painted over. The enterprising Indian Master got closer to the ship and on binocular scrutiny could make out the original painted over name. He alerted the Indian Coast Guard. A Doronier Aircraft was sent on a recce mission and spotted the *Alondra Rainbow*. A Coast Guard ship gave chase and spotted the ship. It refused to heed orders to allow boarding. Two Indian Naval warships (missile boats) were then called in and fired warning shots across the bow. The hijacked ship was boarded and the pirates apprehended. However, for 14 months they could not be tried under the Indian Penal Code because it has no provisions to deal with piracy. They were ultimately tried for armed robbery and sentenced. The IMO is now carrying out a survey of domestic legislation of various countries to identify loopholes. Even though the IMO has produced a plethora of legislation, the enforcement leaves much to be desired. The UNCLOS had adopted the 1958 Geneva Convention's outdated definition of Piracy in its Articles 100-108. These presuppose the pre-existence of two ships and primarily are confined to the acts on the high seas. Since most such incidents are taking place in the coastal waters, the legislation needs revision. The *Alondra Rainbow* incident is illustrative and has many useful lessons. It earned India a lot of gratitude from Japan.

Anti-Piracy Patrols in the Malacca Straits

The menace of Piracy in the Malacca Straits was amply highlighted when in Oct 2001, in the run up to operations against the Taliban and Al Qaida in Afghanistan, the United States requested India to escort high value US ships through the Malacca Straits. The Indian Navy deployed one Off-shore Patrol Vessel (OPV) each for three months at a time to escort US Navy auxillaries like oilers and ammunition ships. In the six months between April and Sep 2002, over 20 such high value ships were escorted between Singapore and the Northern tip of Sumatra. The successful deployment of the Indian OPVs relieved the US Navy from having to spare its fast, high-tech missile armed ship for a slow, low-tech policing role. This has set a major precedent under which Naval warships of various countries could undertake patrols of the threatened, strategic Sea Lines of Communications (SLOCs). Critical choke points that are threatened by terrorist/piratic attacks need to be patrolled on a regular basis. As Vice Admiral GM Hiranandani (Retd) former Vice Chief of the Indian Navy has suggested, this could be undertaken under the auspices of the UNO. Such Naval patrols could be undertaken in the South East Asian waters, off the Coast of Yemen and Somalia and other piracy infested zones. Such armed Naval escorts could go a long way towards curbing the growing menace of piracy and terrorism on the high sea. It is note worthy that the US Coast Gaurd is already providing much escorts to cruise vessells and Cargo carriers entering American ports. Armed patrols of vital SLOCs and choke points like the Mallacca straits would serve to obviate terrorist threat in these critical sea lanes.

Conclusion

Along with America and other Western countries, India too has huge vulnerabilities on the high seas in terms of its merchant marine vessels, its off shore Oil Platforms and its congested Ports. Narcotics smuggling and traditional gun running have been taken over by terrorist networks. Explosives for the Mumbai blasts were smuggled on to the West Coast by small dhows/boats. The Port city of Mumbai which is the commercial capital of India has been particularly vulnerable to repeated terrorist bomb attacks. These have generally been set off in crowded bazaars or trains. However, more specific attacks against ships and ports can not be ruled out. With the mounting threat of terror in and from the sea, India's huge coastline will have to be patrolled, its ports will have to be secured, and a modicum of safety provided to its mercantile fleet. India has a commanding position astride the Indian Ocean and will have a pivotal role to play both in anti-terrorist and anti-piracy operations.India needs to take serious note of the threart of terrorist attacks on its merchant fleet and ports.It needs to adopt a pro-active approach and institute security measures to head off such attacks. It needs to hone its response tools of Vulnerability Assesments and put in place detailed Action Plans.It urgently needs to raise Quick Response Teams and Damage Assesment Teams.Its Ports are a huge vulnerability. Contingency plans must be drawn up to respond to terrorist attacks. We need to focus on Access Control and installation of tracking systems for people, vessels and cargo. We must devise rigorous analytic models and make an all out drive to exploit Commercially Available Off the Shelf Technology. Though action is in hand already, it needs to be speeded up to a level that it anticipates rather than responds to likely terrorist attacks.

Notes

1. Rahul Roy Choudhury "India's Maritime Security" *Knowledge World.* New Delhi. Jun 2000 pp 1.

2. *Ibid* pp 1.

3. *Ibid.* pp 2.

4. *Ibid* pp 20.

5. *Ibid* pp 10.

6. *Ibid.* pp 3.

7. *Ibid.* pp2.

8. *Ibid.* pp 14.

9. *Ibid.* pp 14.

10. *Ibid.* pp 4.

11. US Maritime Transport Committee Report, Jul 2003.

12. NDTV News Telecast Data of Bomb Blasts in 2003.

13. Vice Admiral Prem Vir Das "Maritime Terrorism : Piracy at Sea" Military Year book 2003-04.

14. *Ibid.*

15. *Ibid.*

16. Vice Admiral (Retd.) G M Hiranandani "Patrolling the Indian Ocean". *Indian Defence Review* Apr-Jun 2003. Vol 18 (2) pp 7

17. *Ibid.* pp 8.

‹7›

Technology Resource Multipliers: Combating the Threat

It is imperative that we explore the perfect response options before the terrorist threat on the high seas becomes critical. It would be essential to employ high technology as a force multiplier in the battle against terrorism and piracy on the high seas. This chapter surveys the technological developments in this field by leading companies like the Voyager Systems, Fleet 77, Fortune, Caribbean Satellite Services and Ship Securities etc. A large amount of product information and security solutions are available on the internet. These span the spectrum of Tracking Ship and Container movement (via ship board broadcast transponder systems), Exterior and Interior Cameras and Close Circuit TV systems, sensors and alarms and very innovative electric fences which deliver non-lethal shocks and can secure ships against unauthorised boarding. No discussion of Ship and Port security can be complete without an analysis of the new Biometric technology applications that utilise human characteristics like face recognition, finger print matching, iris and retinal scans, voice analysis, facial thermograms and hand geometry to establish identity and impliment access control. Some of these innovations have been summarised in the succeeding paras.

Terrorist hijackings, Piratic capture and Maritime crimes like "Phantom Ship", involve a seizure of the ship and its diversion from the given route to serve the illegal purpose of its captors. Hence, it is critical that we have a global system to track and monitor the movement of all commercial ships. This should be feasible with the Global Positioning Satellite (GPS) systems now available commercially. Even more critical is the ability of a ship to establish its identity electronically and have an instrument which serves as the equivalent of an airliners black box. (The Voyage Data Recorder)

IMO Responses to Technology

Aline De Bivere writing in the Apr 2001 Issue of the *Ocean Voice* magazine highlighted that after eight years of preparation and debate – the vastly amended Chapter V of the SOLAS Convention came into force on 01 Jul 2002. These amendments are performance related and designed to incorporate advances in Technology related to Ship Board Navigation and greater attention to the human element. In fact, the decision to revise Chapter V is in response to these rapid technological advances. The existing Chapter V of the SOLAS had come into force in the 1980s and has since been overtaken by the rapid leaps in Information Technology and Geographical Information Systems.

The revised Chapter V of the SOLAS Convention has:

- Implications for Ship Design and Operation.
- It contains 35 Regulations (as against the earlier 23).
- Insists on Mandatory Ship Routing Systems (other than traffic separation schemes).
- Mandatory Ship Reporting Systems (other than for Search and Rescue).
- It has called for changes in Bridge Design and the design

and arrangement of Navigation systems and Equipment and Bridge Procedures.

- Provisions on Electronic Chart Display and Information Systems (ECDIS) and Raster Based Chart Display Systems (RCDS).

- The most important amendments pertain to the Installation of Automatic Ship Identification Systems. This is being covered in much greater detail subsequently.

AIS (Automatic Identification System)

AIS is a shipboard broadcast transponder system in which ships continually transmit their ID, position, course, speed and other data to all other nearby ships and shore authorities on a common VHF radio channel. Each ship broadcasts its AIS messages and receives messages from all ships within VHF radio range. AIS messages are updated and retransmitted every few seconds. To achieve this, AIS utilizes a unique Self-Organizing Time-Division Multiple Access (STDMA) data communications scheme. STDMA relies on GPS to provide the universal time reference and ship positioning data needed to synchronize AIS data transmissions from multiple users onto one narrowband channel.

Components of AIS

A shipboard AIS system consists of the following elements:

- An STDMA radio transponder with two VHF receivers and one transmitter (it is also possible that the transponder have a Digital Selective Calling {DSC} receiver tuned to Channel 70).

- A control and display unit, which includes the communications processor and interfaces for taking inputs from the ship's navigation sensors and sending outputs to external systems, such as ECDIS, ARPA, VDR or INMARSAT terminal.

- One or more GPS/DGPS receivers that provide position information as well as the precise time base needed to synchronize the STDMA data transmissions.

AIS is designed to work automatically and continuously in a ship-to-ship mode, but can be switched to an assigned mode for communications with a shore side monitoring station or in a polling mode in which the data transfer occurs in response to interrogation from another ship or shore station.

IMO Requirements

IMO Resolution MSC.74(69), Annex 3 (see Chapter 6) states that an approved shipboard AIS system should be able to perform the following functions:

- Automatically provide information on the ship's identity, type, position, course, speed, navigational status and other safety-related matters to appropriately equipped shore stations, other ships and aircraft.
- Receive automatically such information from similarly fitted ships.
- Monitor and track ships.
- Exchange data with shore-based facilities.

IMO Deadlines

In view of the heightened threat after 9/11, the IMO has laid down specific deadlines for the installation of AIS equipment.

According to SOLAS and its recently approved amendments, AIS equipment must be installed as follows:

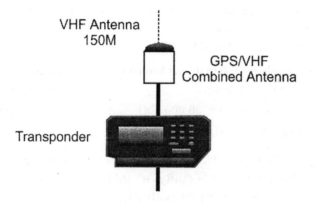

VHF Antenna
150M

GPS/VHF
Combined Antenna

Transponder

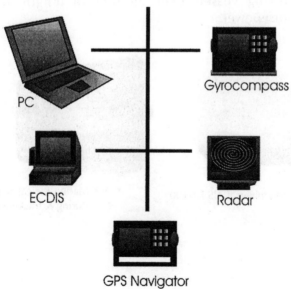

Control and Display Options

PC

Gyrocompass

ECDIS

Radar

GPS Navigator

Ships Constructed on or after July 1, 2002	Deadline
Passenger ships	July 1, 2002
Ships between 300 and 500 GRT on International voyages only	July 1, 2002
Cargo ships greater than 500 GRT	July 1, 2002
Retrofit Vessels on International Voyages	**Deadline**
Passenger ships and tankers	July 1, 2003
Other vessels greater than 50,000 GRT	July 1, 2004
Other vessels 300 - 50,000 GRT	Dec 31, 2004

In addition, the U.S. Congress is mandating under the Marine Transportation Security Act (MTSA) that the following vessels must be equipped with AIS:

- All commercial self-propelled vessels over 65 feet in length.
- Towing vessels over 26 feet in length and 600 horsepower.

- Furuno Universal AIS FA-100

- MX-Marine (Leica) MX420/AIS Monitoring & tracking ships

- Any vessel carrying more passengers for hire as determined by the U.S. Coast Guard.

- Any other vessel for which AIS is deemed necessary for safe navigation of the vessel as determined by the U.S. Coast Guard.

- MX420/AIS Position Display

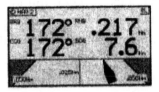

- MX420/AIS Steering Display

AIS Modes

Ship-to-Ship

The primary operating mode for AIS will be automatic ship-to-ship reporting, where each ship transmits its data to all other AIS-equipped ships within VHF range. Position and other data are fed from the ship's sensors into the AIS system, where the data is formatted and transmitted in a short data burst on a dedicated VHF channel. When received on the other ships, the data is decoded and displayed for the officer of the watch in graphic and text format for all other AIS-equipped ships within range.

Gyrocompass   ECDIS   GPS Navigator   Radar

- Available displays with Furuno AIS system

The AIS data may also be fed to the ship's integrated navigation systems and radar plotting systems to provide AIS tags for radar targets, or be logged to the ship's Voyage Data Recorder (VDR) for playback and future analysis.

Updated AIS messages are transmitted every few seconds, to keep the information up to date. Note that the ship-to-ship data exchange takes place automatically without any action required by the watch officer on either ship.

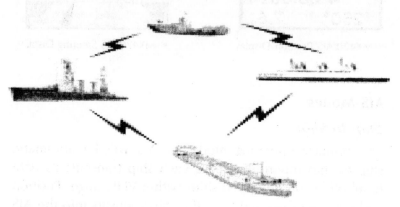

Shore side Monitoring

In coastal waters, shore side authorities may establish automated AIS stations to monitor the movement of vessels through the area. These stations may simply monitor AIS transmissions from passing ships, or may actively poll vessels

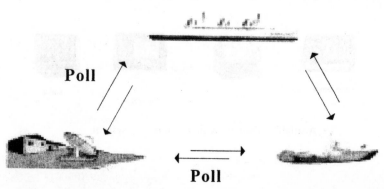

Data Type	Static	Voyage related	Dynamic	Safety-related
Description	IMO number	Ship's Hazardous Cargo (type)	Ship's position accuracy indi- and integenty status	Sent as needed
	Call sign			
	Name	Destination & ETA	Time in UTC course & speed over ground	
	Length			
	Beam	(at master's description)	Heading new-gational status (e.g. at anchor, not under command manually entered)	
			Rate of turn	
Source	Programmed into the unit at commissioning	Entered manually by the master via password protected routine	Development ship's GPS and other sensors	Inserted at any time by the ship or shore station
Transmission Rate	Every Six minutes or on polled by shore station speed		Depends on ship status and	As needed

For the Dynamic column under Transmission Rate:

At anchor	3 min
0-14 knots	10 sec
0-14 knots cc	3.5 sec
14-23 knots	6 sec
14-23 knots cc	2 sec
23+ knots	2 sec
23+ knots cc	2 sec

cc = changing course

Model Chart of Information Available Through AIS

via the AIS channels, requesting data such as identification, destination, ETA, type of cargo and other information. Coast stations can also use the AIS channels for shore-to-ship transmissions, to send information on tides, notices to mariners and local weather forecasts. Multiple AIS coast stations and repeaters may be tied together into Wide Area Networks (WAN) for extended coverage.

VDR - Voyage Data Recorder

Similar to the black boxes of air crafts, VDRs or Voyage Data Recorders are now being installed on ships to get quick results for accident investigation, consequent data acquisition and evaluation, new experiences and daily usage of incoming data. Designed accordingly with the Regulators laid down by IMO/IEC/EC, the system consists of a dedicated PC, system rack with a range of sensors as required. Electronics main unit contains the computer and interconnection interfaces. Thus data from myriad sources including bridge equipment (interfaced), audio/video sensors and hull stress detectors etc. is recorded as incident

A Voyage Data Recorder; *Courtesy:* Rutter Technologies Inc.

data . Incident data can be saved and later loaded on to a PC for analysis. Thus data can be retreived after a major accident or say, a terrorist strike, still intact. Data can also be viewed in real time, and there is the option of incorporating this new feature onto existing EPIRBs (Emergency Position Indicating Radio Beacons- a float free device which is able to alert via satellite shore authorities in case of emergencies and also able to transmit its location for rescue purposes.) This technology can now also be utilised to monitor proceedings on a vessel remotely from shore. Such features could be crucial in cases like highjackings etc.

Features

A typical VDR will record and store at aleast 12 hrs of:

- Radar
- Bridge audio (Conversations on the bridge)
- Communications audio (VHF, HF radio etc.)
- Position
- Heading
- Course
- Speed
- Depth
- Date and time (UTC) Shaft RPM
- Engine order and response
- Rudder order and response
- Wind speed and direction
- Fire alarm system
- Watertight door / fire door status

- Main alarms system outputs
- Hull openings status
- Hull stress and Accelerations monitoring

Final Recording Medium

The data is stored in the "Final Recording Medium, FRM" with location aid devices. The data is stored in the main system and optional also in a float-free capsule, an EPIRB amongst other things

Some features include:

- Recording of last 12 hours data
- Push button "SAVE DATA."
- As simple as possible to operate
- Local copies of incident data
- A fixed or float-free capsule
- Withstand shock, penetration by a 250 KG pin dropped 3 m.
- Fire for 10 hours
- Submergence to 6000 metres
- Acoustic beacon

EPIRB and VDR - Voyage Data Recorder Add-On

The figure depicts an EPIRB which has been extended by the following functions:

Tron VDR-GMDSS EPIRB with Voyage Data Recorder storage controller
Courtesy: Rutter Technologies Inc.

- Integrated data server to store the acquired VDR data
- At least 4 gigabyte hard disk memory for duplication of data stored in the system main memory
- Standard Ethernet interface (10BaseT) with integrated automatic hydrostatic release for float free operation

Other features which make up a VDR include the following (based on the Rutter RD100 model):

Data Management Unit (DMU)

This consists of a rack-mounted Pentium PC (contains Data Acquisition and management software, radar interface cards, audio data acquisition cards, input ports for NMEA-0183 / IEC 61162 data and a LAN connection for soft downloading).

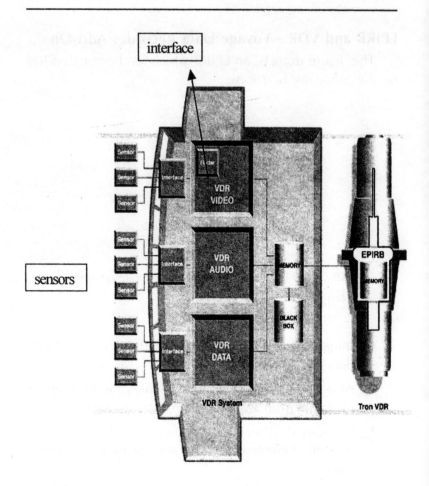

Radar Interface

This interface is a PC-based software and hardware system designed to capture high resolution RGB images at 15-second intervals. Optionally, shorter intervals can be accommodated.

Bridge Audio

The base unit includes six surface-mountable microphones, preamplifiers and multi-channel mixers, and allows for continuous recording. The audio system is easily expanded

Radio Communications Audio

One radio input is provided for continuous recording of transmit and receive audio from either VHF or HF radio (easily expanded).

NMEA-0183 / IEC 61162 Data

Special data multiplexers are provided to allow for recording of 16 data inputs at one-second intervals (easily expanded to accept more inputs).

DMU Removable Storage

This consists of a removable hard drive mounted in the PC. A lock secures this storage.

Recording Duration

The minimum recording duration is 12 hours, based on the sample intervals required by IMO. This is easily expanded.

UPS

The uninterruptible power supply (UPS) is configured to run off 220VAC / 50Hz (unit is capable of powering the VDR for the purpose of recording for a period of at least two hours in the event of a loss of external power).

Soft Downloading System

A 100 megabit/second ethernet LAN connection is available for soft downloading of the data to a PC, without interrupting the recording. This data can be stored on a variety of media for future playback.

Playback Software

A software package is supplied to allow immediate playback and viewing of the downloaded data. NMEA data is available on a serial port for output to electronic chart ECDIS systems or a simulator.

VDR Alarm Display

An external audio and visual alarm unit for alerting of an error condition in the VDR is included (alarm can be silenced).

Hardened Storage Unit (FRM)

A protective capsule containing the Final Recording Medium and meeting all the requirements of IMO is included.

Sensor Interfaces

Special sensor interfaces are available to convert non NMEA 0183 / IEC 61162 data to this format. Typical sensor interfaces include gyro-compass, rudder order/response, engine order/response, wind speed and direction and shaft/engine rpm.

Real-Time Display

A real-time display of the NMEA-0183 / IEC 61162 data being recorded can be provided.

Remote Data Access

Onboard data is accessible for remote display and download via a satellite communications link

IMO Requirements

IMO Regulation 20 - Voyage Data Recorders (VDR)

1. To assist in casualty investigations, ships, when engaged on international voyages, subject to the provisions

of regulation 1.4, shall be fitted with a Voyage Data Recorder (VDR) as follows:

* passenger ships constructed on or after 1 July 2002;

* ro-ro passenger ships constructed before 1 July 2002 not later than the first annual survey after 1 July 2002;

* passenger ships, other than ro-ro passenger ships, constructed before 1 July 2002 not later than 1 January 2004; and

* all ships other than passenger ships of 3,000 gross tonnage and upwards constructed on or after 1 July 2002

IMO Fitting Requirements

Thus, a VDR Is to be carried by a vessel in international voyages:

• Ro-ro passenger ferries

• Ships >2999T

• Passenger ships

• Ships with hazardous cargo such as tankers

Thus the VDR will now be able to provide crucial evidence/ or real time data for the purposes of loss prevention, incident reconstruction and help in combating / developing measures against maritime crime, accidents etc. and promote safety and security at sea.

Cameras and Monitoring

The ISPS Code requires ships to monitor and control access and activities of people and cargo. The goal is to provide enhanced watch keeping of the ship's exterior and interior, including key access points and strategic onboard areas. Also required is the ability to review, record and archive images and data.

This requirement can be met with exterior and interior cameras and micro-sensors, coupled with closed-circuit television (CCTV) components to enable viewing, recording and archiving of images and data.

While surveillance systems for port facility perimeters is a familiar sight, it would be worth while taking a look at what some leading market players have to offer for vessels.

Exterior Cameras:

Voyager Systems for eg., offer bulletproof, all-weather cameras to provide excellent images in a wide variety of light conditions, (including low light and against bright light). These cameras can be installed at all ship access doors and hatches. Although the cameras are fixed, they provide up to 360° surveillance and can be controlled with an easy-to-use keypad, including pan, tilt, zoom, focus, panning angle and speed, and automatic preset positions. Such cameras provide technology intensive surveillance solutions without adding to manpower or additional man hours requirements.

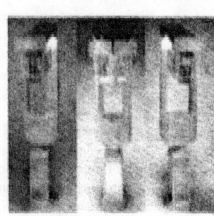

AUTO PLANNING

Interior Cameras: A variety of interior camera types are available to meet distance and lighting requirements in key passageways and stairwells of ships. Interior access cameras can provide video coverage of all access doors, hatches, and passageways.

CCTV Components for Viewing, Recording & Archiving:

Full motion video of both exterior and interior cameras is displayed at a monitoring station on the bridge. Camera views can also be displayed on all vessel TV's with just a little additional cost.

The standard monitoring station includes one 42" screen, which is split into multiple panes for monitoring views from different cameras. Also included is one 20" screen (i.e. Workstation) with an easy-to-use controller keypad.

This system allows the operator to zoom-in to a specific camera, and freeze-frame or rewind the video for

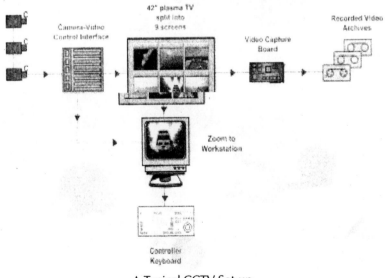

A Typical CCTV Set up
(Source: Voyager Systemic)

analysis. It also provides maximum control of every interior and exterior camera, including: pan, tilt, zoom, focus, panning angle & speed, and automatic preset positions. This system therefore provides a very user friendly solution for ship based surveillance tanks.

Finally, this monitoring system enables onboard digital video recording, which can be set up to be automatic, triggered by sensors/alarms, and/or activated manually. System can also be configured to archive video recordings on a periodic basis (i.e. remove from hard drive and

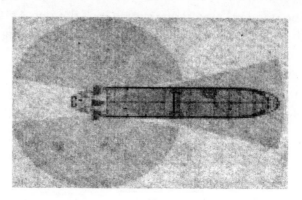

• Exterior cameras mounted on ship can provide local or wide areas of surveillance coverage.

• Elbex EX600, EXU12 and EX8000 series interior cameras.

Communications

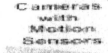

Cameras
with
Motion
Sensors

**Video Data
Alarms**

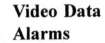

Cameras
and
Monitoring

Sensors
and
Alarms

Interior & Exterior
Microwave Sensors

 42″ Monitor split
into multiple

Interior Audible
Alarm

 20″ Workstation

Exterior Audible
Alarm

Controller
keyboard

Visible
Alarms

Recorded Video

transfer to storage). Such video recording/capture of data would be useful aids during projection of the culprits concerned and also provide excellent training material. Manufactures claim that exterior or interior cameras provide real time surveillance/monitoring capabilities without enhancing the manpower requirements. The 42" screen (split into multiple passes for monitoring views from different cameras) could be installed either in the Bridge or a central location eg Masters quarters for round the clock monitoring.

Sensors and Alarms

In addition to opitical and video sensors, Microwave sensors are mounted in key passageways, stairwells, and deck areas. Outdoor units are designed to withstand the most severe environmental conditions. All units incorporate tamper-proof housing.

These sensors use advanced signal processing to ignore birds and randomly moving objects. An internal sensitivity switch allows custom settings for the distance an intruder must move to initiate an alarm. Thus, these sensors offer the sensitivity and flexibility to ensure a high level of security while virtually eliminating false alarms.

All sensors are connected to the central monitoring station on the bridge. This central station can control settings and operation for each unit independently based on vessel surroundings and operation (i.e. at port, at sea, other vessel traffic, etc.). Notification of intruder motion can be configured for visual and/or audible alarms, both on the bridge and at multiple remote locations (e.g. Master's Quarters). Manual activation buttons for visual and/ or audible alarms can be installed on the bridge and at multiple remote locations. Sensors also come with a Pager to notify watch stander of area intrusions.

- A selection of ProTech sensors, include

  — the Piramid HS Interior
  Intruder Detector

  — the Stereo Doppler

- Explosion-proof Microwave
  Exterior Intruder Detector

  — the Piramid XL Exterior
  Detector with Sounder.

- Microwave sensors can be configured to detect intrusion from 90 feet away.

Security Systems

The ISPS Code requires ships to maintain a minimum level of security, to respond to a security threat and to operate while under attack. (For a more complete summary of these three requirements and their sources, refer to the ISPS Code for details).

The key capabilities required are:

- Earliest possible detection of threat.
- Deterrence measures.
- Communications capability in secure zones (onboard ship) in case of attack.

Voyager Systems offers 3 basic packages that meets these requirements. These packages were developed by this company to conform to the guidelines and enable the procedures outlined in the IMO circular MSC/Circ.623 (May 2002).

Standard Packages

Equipment	Package 1	Package 2	Package 3
AIS System (Required by IMO)	X	X	X
Voyage Data Recorder (Required by IMO)	X	X	X
Fleet 77 (GMDSS Approved)		X	X
Fleet Tracking			X
Rotating Search Lights			X
Interior Access Area Cameras	X	X	X
Microwave Sensors (4)	X	X	X
External Camera Port Facing Forward	X	X	X
External Camera Stbd Facing Forward	X	X	X
External Camera Center Facing Forward		X	X
External Camera Port Anchor Hawse Pipe			X

External Camera Stbd Anchor Hawse Pipe		X
External Camera Port Facing Aft	X	X
External Camera Stbd Facing Aft	X	X
Onboard Digital Video Recording X	X	X
Camera Motion Sensors	X	X

Each of these packages is made up of components from basically 3 types of equipment:

- Communications.
- Cameras and Monitoring.
- Sensors and Alarms.

These are some of the standard packages offered by Voyager System and other firms. The companies concerned are also helping the Ship crews to adapt these new devices with the normal ship operations.

Options

1. FLIR night vision auto tracking security camera.
2. Additional location(s) for security control panel and monitors.
3. Additional Fleet77 system for live high-speed video and ship's administration.
4. Remote site monitoring and archiving of data.
5. 24/7 service contract.

Complete security systems include Communications, Cameras & Monitoring, and Sensors & Alarms.

Communications

The ISPS Code requires a Ship Security Alert System that can transmit ship-to-shore security alerts—including ship ID, location and a security message—and a system that can be activated from the bridge and at least one other location.

This requirement can be met with a Fleet 77 or Inmarsat C communications system.

Fleet 77

Fleet 77 provides an integrated, on-line communications hub which links to and operates through the ship's fax machines, phones and computers:

- It is Compatible with onboard PBX and computer networks and (IP/LAN, WAN, VPN).
- Provides Continuous real-time access to needed information.
- Provides Reliable and secure digital communications.

The basic package consists of a transceiver and antenna, together with a handset and cradle. The lightweight and compact equipment is relatively easy to install. What requires finesse is linking the Fleet 77 to the ship's onboard fax, phones and computers to produce an integrated system that is actually reliable. This in effect offers an ideal networked solutions that enhances connectivity.

The Fleet 77 system provides continuous two-way communications via Inmarsat satellites. It allows the ship to stay in-touch 24 hours a day with onshore management systems via the Web, including full e-mail and Internet services from all shipboard PCs set up as part of the network.

Fleet 77 also offers flexibility and low-cost by using MPDS communications technology. MPDS packages data so that it is sent in small packets through channels shared by other users. Individual users are charged only for the amount of data they actually send, not for the time spent online. This means ships can stay online all the time and end up with much lower costs than with traditional log-in programmes.

MPDS also enables LANs and VPNs to furnish ships at sea constant access to knowledge bases, filing systems, notice boards, communication media, and even e-commerce. Position reporting, electronic charts, weather reports, maintenance schedules and automatic equipment & machinery surveillance reports can now be transmitted and received as if the ship was in the office next door. Fleet 77 also handles the transmission of larger documents and files (e.g. videoconferencing, streaming video, live video feed, and large photo transmission) through direct ISDN connection.

Inmarsat C

Inmarsat C provides a more cost-effective solution, consisting of a single transceiver unit. It delivers global Inmarsat C mobile communications and can be configured to provide:

- 2-way data, fax, and e-mail communications worldwide.
- Data-and position reporting to multiple destinations and time intervals.

- Thrane & Thrane TT-3084A Capsat© Fleet77

- Fleet77 also enables live video and video conferencing.

- 24-hr communications via the Web, including e-mail, and linked to onboard fax, phones and computers.

- Thrane & Thrane TT-3020C Capsat© Transceiver

- Pre-programming of DNID's for global coverage
- Connection to multiple printers and remote alarms.

Info Technology

For ease-of-use and consistency of appearance increasing numbers of applications, databases and services, including marine software applications are becoming web-based. Unfortunately users often have to manage multiple passwords for each application logon some of which have to be changed frequently creating a climate in which passwords are written down or chosen poorly. As a result application security is compromised. A large number of calls received by help desks are from users who forget their password. Applications that require databases of users and access policies, often have administrators whose sole task is to synchronise names, passwords and roles across those multiple applications and user directories. Built-in access control mechanisms available in existing products are often too complex or not scalable enough to meet the cross-force boundary needs of joined up maritime business and databases. E- commerce is coming in a big way into the maritime industry, with major business and administrative transactions occuring online. Even private ship owning companies carry out most of their technical communication over the net. Planned maintenance systems, procurement systems, accounting and billing systems, voyage sensitive info, cargo details are all dealt with online today by most shipping companies. It is also likely that with developments in cyber applications there might be applications like 'e-crewing' and national databases on whose basis crew employments be made. In the light of these developments, the potential of terrorist friendly parties hacking into databases and cyber applications with an intention of fudging records, gaining access to restricted informaion or stalling operations etc, is going to grow at a proportional rate to these new applications themselves. Thus there is a need to establish an environment of 'e-security' in the present maritime cyberworld. "Thanks to recent innovations in security it is possible to provide a secure 'tunnel' through the Internet", explains Richard Mardling, Business Development Manager at Enline. Shipping companies opting for secure networks is a positive prognosis measure. The Virtual Private Network has tremendous potential for all businesses", commented Richard Mardling. "The ability to establish an effective and secure connection within hours means that many organisations can now consider remote connections to their network for the first time". Browser access controllers including those relying on smart cards and biometrics, firewalls and routers etc. are the bywords of a secure e-business of tomorrow. Though not readily apparent, there is potential risk for shipping companies and other maritime interests busy carrying out commerce on the internet. This issue should, however be addressed as soon as possible.

Fleet tracking softwares

This is software owners will want to use to track and communicate with their ship or whole fleet. Simple to setup and use will give one wealth of available information and options.

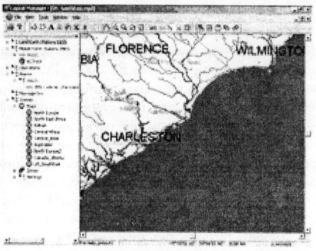

Windows based tracking software TT-10220C Capsat Manager
Courtesy: Almex Marine Ltd.

Capsat Manager is a Windows based fleet tracking program that enables you to track your vehicles, wherever they are, via the Inmarsat-C system. Capsat Manager communicates to Thrane & Thrane Inmarsat-C Land Earth Stations via either PSTN, ISDN, X.25 or the Internet. This is a client/server based program, operating as a multi-user or stand-alone system.

Position reports and data received from a mobile are stored in an Microsoft Access database. Retrieval of these data is done easily by using ODBC, for example for SCADA applications E-mails can be sent to your vehicles, using Microsoft Outlook in multi-user environments or Microsoft Outlook Express in stand-alone applications. You can set and control automatic vehicles position reporting from the Capsat Manager, or request a position report whenever needed.

Specific groups of vehicles can be surveyed by individual users using the "operations" facility.

Monitoring and control handling of incoming alarms from the vehicles, containers and ships can be done directly in the Capsat Manager.

Several geographical areas can be monitored at the same time.

Features

* Full featured Fleet tracking program, supporting Landmobile, Maritime and Aeronautical position reports.
* Internet access to mobiles (ships/vehicles) saves landline costs.
* Easy messaging to and from the mobile using e-mail.
* Detailed maps show mobile positions and trails on an ordinary PC.
* Excellent zooming facilities due to vector map material.
* User defined Go or No-go zones applicable for each mobile.

Ships Security Alert System

By middle of 2004 ships from following categories will have to comply with SSAS (Ships Security Alert System) requirements: -

- Passenger ships
- Cargo ships of 500 or more GT
- Mobile offshore drilling units

One example of a ship security alert system integrated unto the existing sat- c equipment is Almex Marine Ltd.'s 2 solutions claimed to be not expensive or complicated to install and use.

For example, the Ship Security Alert System is based upon the well-known and reliable Inmarsat-C technology, which for more than a decade has been part of the Global Maritime Distress and Safety System. The System is approved by by Inmarsat, which means that any alert sent from the Ship Security Alert System will be handled with the same priority and reliability as a Distress alert sent via the GMDSS system.

The standard TT-3000SSAS Capsat(r) Ship Security Alert System package (from Almex., see www.almexmarine.com) consist of a easyTrack unit with a 20 meter transceiver cable and an interconnection box. Besides that, two alarm buttons and one test button that can be installed up to 50 meters away from the interconnection box are included. Most modernship security alert systems based on Inmarsat-c consist of these components. Two alarm buttons are located strategically on the vessel, one on the bridge and the other in the Ship security Officer's cabin (or as per the location decided by the installers etc.).

Keeping track of the vessel at all times is also possible by activating position polling, The easyTrack is then capable of reporting its GPS position to a network of your choice at given intervals.

Features
* SOLAS Regulation XI-2/6
* Based on the existing Inmarsat-C service
* Total flexibility in routing to e-mail addresses, anti piracy centres, GSM phones, Fax and Telex.

Other upgrade for users with existing Inmarsat-c:

Ship Security Alert Add-On

Owners of existing Inmarsat TT-3020C transceivers are able to purchase a kit and get SSAS software to make for SSAS requirement.

The solution offers easy installation to the Capsat transceiver via ARCNET with twisted pair cable. Floating 10.5-32 VDC power supply and full compliance with Inmarsat CN137bis Covert/Security Alert requirements.

SHIPLOC

SHIPLOC is a small satellite-tracking device concealed on ships which allows owners to monitor the movement of their vessels.

The Ship loc system operates in two modes:-

Normal Mode Operations: Under normal conditions, SHIPLOC is an owner-friendly ship tracking system. A ship owner, can have access to the position of his vessel on the SHIPLOC Web site, via email, or using a dedicated software called **Elsa**. Accessing the data will enable you to check that ships are on their expected course and will indicate if they will arrive at their destination on time.

Crisis Mode Operations: When the owner learns of a piracy attack, he immediately alerts the IMB piracy reporting center in Kuala Lumpur, at any time of day or night. The IMB piracy center, after accessing the ship's position data, will alert the local law enforcement agencies and coordinate all necessary action to ensure the safety of the crew and recovery of the ship.

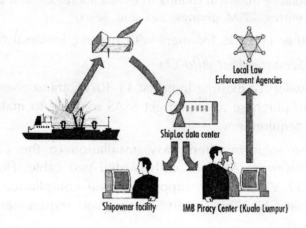

Satellite Based Cargo Container Intrusion Monitoring And Reporting System

From ship security perse, let in new study the vital aspect of containers Security. As stated earlier, over 16 million containers are moved all over the globe each year. There constitute a huge vulnerability which terrorists could easily exploit. Contanier security today consititues the most vulnerable and exposed flank of sea borne commerce.

For several years technology has been evolving to the state that simple cost effective technology solutions are available for many of today's business issues. Just as the internet has become a vital component of electronic commerce, wireless data systems will provide an information network in near real time regarding the movements of containerized cargo security.

The US Department of Defense Global Positioning System (GPS) is one of these enabling technologies that can pinpoint the location of an item anywhere on the planet within 100 meters. Coupled with wireless communications systems both terrestrial and satellite based, valuable location and intrusion information can be transmitted to the appropriate authorities. Small transceivers that can send and receive signals from packetized data cellular systems, when available, or toggle over to Low Earth Orbit (LEO) satellites, are attached to intermodal shipping containers. Sensors are installed to record information regarding numerous parameters, temperature, shock, weight, motion, combined with GPS receiver information and container door intrusion devices.

A shipment is loaded and sealed and a phone call to the network control center 800 number begins the tracking and monitoring process. From this point any opening of the container will be considered an unauthorized intrusion unless a Customs (or other authorized) agent inspection code is recorded at the control center. When the container arrives at its destination another brief message signals the monitoring service is ended.

An unauthorized entry into a container can be signaled via land based or satellite based communications. The control center then automatically notifies pre-selected authorities or agents to act on the owners behalf and prevent the theft if possible.

The industry benefits by having a new technology solution that can increase preventive measures, thereby reducing loss. In the event that the loss occurs, a timely recovery effort aided by location information, has the potential of reducing losses by pinpointing recovery activities.

The in-transit (SMART CONTAINER) cargo security system accurately records information prior to, and immediately after an unauthorized intrusion incident which will provide surveyors and claims adjustors incident time, date, and location information that is currently not easily determined.

A number of insurance groups have indicated use of advanced cargo theft prevention technology would qualify for considerable insurance premium savings. This technology is appropriate for high value and high risk shipments.

There will be efforts to overcome these security measures and it should be stated clearly that tracking and monitoring systems do not provide a panacea. However as those efforts increase, wireless data technologies are advancing rapidly and will provide a nimble opponent to cargo thieves, and terrorist infiltrators.

Intrusion Detection Systems (IDS)

Principles of Operation

The devices detect intrusion through the use of sound, vibration, temperature change, movement, electrical disturbance, light beams and broken circuits. The main component of the intrusion detection system is the response. If no one can hear the signal or alarm, then no one can respond. The alarm signal can be sounded by an external warning horn or it can be sent to a central receiving station. In many cases both actions will occur. For the manned vessel, the IDS can send a silent alarm to the watch crew or on duty security personnel.

Intrusion detection devices use a variety of methods to detect intrusion. Not all of these methods are compatible with the marine environment and vessel operations. The following methods of detection are applicable to vessel security requirements, and they will be discussed in detail regarding advantages and disadvantages:

- Breaking an electric circuit (switches).
- Making an electric circuit (pressure pads).
- Interrupting or disturbing a light beam (photoelectric).
- Detecting sounds.
- Detecting motion (ultrasonic motion sensors).
- Electronic Perimeter Defense (RADAR).
- Duress alarms (operated by personnel).
- Closed Circuit Television (CCTV).

Intrusion detection systems can be configured to report security breaches locally, such as notifying the watch crew onboard, or they can remotely notify security personnel or police, as in the case of an unmanned vessel. The latter type is known as a Central Station Alarm System. A combination of the two can also be employed if needed.

Electric Fence: A high-voltage electric fence for ships is the latest weapon to be endorsed by ICC's International Maritime Bureau (IMB) in the worldwide fight against piracy.

The 9,000-volt fence, designed to protect a ship's deck, is currently being tested by Secure-Ship, a Dutch security company.

Deployment of the fence onto the worldwide shipping market came just a week before the release of ICC's Annual Piracy Report, which was expected to show a significant increase in pirate attacks on the world's oceans.

Devised to protect both a ship's cargo and its crew, the fence is being hailed by experts as a breakthrough in maritime security.

"Creating an impenetrable barrier of safety around a ship's perimeter is a goal which manufacturers have been pursuing for years," explained International Maritime Bureau (IMB) Director, Captain Pottengal Mukundan. "The majority of previous products of this nature proved incapable of offering a ship both safety and utility simultaneously. This fence strikes that perfect balance, allowing ship captains to protect their vessels from pirate attacks without having to arm themselves."

The Secure-Ship system comprises a collapsible electric fence mounted around a ship's deck. Crew members can activate port and/or starboard zones, allowing work to take place on one side of the ship while the fence is charged on the other.

A sophisticated control module detects entry attempts and activates lights, alarms, and sirens to alert crew.

The electric fence delivers a 9,000 volt shock at any point of contact—a painful but not deadly charge. The manufacturers say their system has been designed to operate in all types of weather and is not hindered by salt-water spray.

"All but the most determined pirates will quickly take their activities elsewhere when faced with an electric fence," said Captain Mukundan. "This anti-boarding device will also prevent stowaways, deterring illegal immigration and possibly thwarting would-be terrorists".

The IMB says the introduction of the Secure-Ship system is being well received by the industry.

However, the presence of electrically charged wires means the system cannot be used on oil tankers or other ships carrying heavily flammable materials.

The Secure-Ship electric fence is the latest anti-piracy device to be endorsed by the IMB, the maritime crime fighting arm of ICC, the world business organization. With more than 8,000 member companies in over 140 countries, ICC is the world's largest, most representative business association.

Two other important security measures advocated by the IMB include the satellite-tracking system SHIPLOC and recent international legislation requiring all ships to have their International Maritime Organization (IMO) number visibly embossed on their hulls.

The embossing of IMO numbers is a requirement of the new International Ship and Port Facility Code (ISPS), implemented within the Safety of Life at Sea (SOLAS) Convention.

IMB expects this new legislation will improve transparency of identity and improve the tracing of hijacked vessels.

Access Control

A furore was created the world over when the US Department of Homeland Security announced that from Jan 2004 on wards, citizens of all (but some 21 specified countries) entering the United States would be finger printed and screened for biometric indices. These will be instanty matched with computer data files of the biometric characterstics of all known known terrorists—o their sympathisers. The whole process, it was claimed would take no more then 15 to 20 seconds.

As has been highlighted earlier access control to ports and ships is now a vital aspect of Security. This can be achieved by means of :-

- Bio-metric Cards. These scan biological specifics like finger prints or irises of the eye and ensure detection of unauthorised personel.

- Surveillance Systems like the Close Circuit TV Cameras and Ultrasound scanners can be installed on ships and Port facility perimeters.

Biometric Systems

This Chapter includes a broad survey of the state of the Art systems new available for ensuring ship Security. Technology is now in a position to provide credible force multipliers that can defeat terrorist/pirate attacks on Sea and in ports

Biometrics

Biometrics today is a fast emerging technology which could have the single most significant impact on the human access control and surveillance requirements of port facilities and ships. This technology is already invading security systems established in Airport environments, industrial /business establishments and government facilities with futuristic models claiming that within the next decade, carrying a biometric identity would be as common as a credit card - as this technolgy will soon find its applications in all spheres of life including day to day shopping , travelling and finding your access to services, products and establishments.

Biometrics refers to the automatic identification of a person based on his/her physiological or behavioral characteristics. A biometric system is essentially a pattern recognition system which makes a personal identification by determining the authenticity of a specific physiological or behavioral characteristic possessed by the user. To date, the technology is most effective as an identification tool capable of distilling large databases down to a smaller gallery of possible matches.

This method of identification is preferred over traditional methods involving passwords, PIN numbers and photo id for various reasons:

(i) The person to be identified is required to be physically present at the point-of-identification;

(ii) Identification based on biometric techniques obviates the need to remember a password or carry a token. PINs and passwords may be forgotten

(iii) Token based methods of identification like passports, driver's licenses, crew/ stevedore ID may be forged, stolen, or lost.

With the increased use of computers as vehicles of information technology, it is necessary to restrict access to sensitive/personal data. By replacing PINs, biometric techniques can potentially prevent unauthorized access to or fraudulent use of ATMs, cellular phones, smart cards, desktop PCs, workstations, and computer networks. Moreover, biometrics can be used as extremely effective tools for surveillance and access control systems- and help to detect suspicious movements of unauthorised personnel or even terrorists in the area of interest. Thus biometric systems of identification are enjoying a renewed interest. Various types of biometric systems are being used for real-time identification, the most popular are based on face recognition and fingerprint matching. However, there are other biometric systems that utilize iris and retinal scan, speech, facial thermograms, and hand geometry.

A brief overview of these technologies available would give one a better picture of their applicability in the marine environment

Facial recognition (FR)

Facial recognition technology - which originated in the mathematics of advanced satellite image processing - enables one-to-many identification searches (1:n) and one-to-one verification matches (1:1).

The technology consists of a series of components packaged within a Software Development Kit (SDK). These components find faces within a digital photograph or video stream and match those images to like-looking facial images stored within a database. Facial recognition involves three core steps, regardless of the specific implementation of the technology.

Create an Encode Array from any facial image

The algorithm examines the face, and generates a mathematical description expressed as a 1024 byte string. During the enrollment process, this encode array is linked to a unique identifier for the facial image.

Compare a Probe Encode Array to a Stored Encode Array in a database

The facial recognition server searches an in-memory database of Encode Arrays and calculates a percentage confidence indicator for each match.

Present Results

The facial recognition server presents a gallery of database images in order of match confidence.

Modern facial recognition packages are progressing more and more with improvements in multiple simultaneous image capturing operations, face labelling and tracking through observed spaces, expanding databases of "persons of interest"- effectively meaning that these can now be used as surveillance and access control equipment with increasing accuracy.

Latest developments are also being made in the component of real-time querying of text- and image-based information from disparate data sources, including multiple Records Management Systems (RMS), Jail Management Systems (JMS), and other criminal justice and public safety databases. The software also enables querying between multiple jurisdictions and agencies.

For each agency, the system presents itself as a series of highly-customizable, browser-based modules that can be assembled easily to meet the specific needs of each user. Moreover, as the data sharing network adds new information resources, they can be added to the system and accessed over the same network. The network can be expanded and databases increased with advanced

Facial Recognition and Proximity Access Controller offered by Ohana International which can store up to 7,800 Facial Images

intelligence sharing between intergovermental agencies. Such software solutions are already available for eg. Inforce is a software company which develops softwares such as Inforce justice suit which offers amongst other things, XML-based data sharing across regions and between systems, searches enhanced with facial recognition, intelligence access from multiple ODBC, OLEDB, and legacy databases with a single query etc. This provides the user with the tool to recognise criminals and terrorists whose records are available with another agency in some other part of the world. Thus other than identity verification, the device is able to isolate people in a crowd who appear to look like any subject in the the 'person of interest' database.

Fingerprint Matching

Among all the biometric techniques, fingerprint-based identification is the oldest method which has been successfully used in numerous applications. Everyone is known to have unique, immutable fingerprints. A fingerprint is made of a series of ridges and furrows on the surface of the finger. The uniqueness of a fingerprint can be determined by the pattern of ridges and furrows as well as the minutiae points. Minutiae points are local ridge characteristics that occur at either a ridge bifurcation or a ridge ending.

Fingerprint matching techniques can be placed into two categories: minutae-based and correlation based. Minutiae-based techniques first find minutiae points and then map their relative placement on the finger. The correlation-based method is able to overcome some of the difficulties of the minutiae-based approach. Correlation-based techniques require the precise location of a registration point and are affected by image translation and rotation.

Fingerprint matching is a common sight

Large volumes of fingerprints are collected and stored everyday in a wide range of applications including forensics, access control, and driver license registration. An automatic recognition of people based on fingerprints requires that the input fingerprint be matched with a large number of fingerprints in a database (FBI database contains approximately 70 million fingerprints!). To reduce the search time and computational complexity, it is desirable to classify these fingerprints in an accurate and consistent manner so that the input fingerprint is required to be matched only with a subset of the fingerprints in the database. Modern package focus on these and are now very effective.

Hand Geometry

This approach uses the geometric shape of the hand for authenticating a user's identity. Authentication of identity using hand geometry is an interesting problem. Individual hand features are not descriptive enough for identification. However, it is possible to devise a method by combining various individual features to attain robust verification. For some kinds of access control like immigration and border control, passenger ship access, invasive biometrics (eg., fingerprints) may not be desirable as they infringe on privacy. In such situations it is desirable to have a biometric system that is sufficient for verification. As hand geometry is not distinctive, it is the ideal choice. Furthermore, hand geometry data is easier to collect. With fingerprint collection good frictional skin is required by imaging systems, and with retina-based recognition systems, special lighting is necessary. Additionally, hand geometry can be easily combined with other biometrics, namely fingerprint. One can envision a system where fingerprints are used for (infrequent) identification and hand geometry is used for (frequent) verification.

Speech-recognition and speaker-verification systems

The speaker-specific characteristics of speech are due to differences in physiological and behavioral aspects of the speech production system in humans. The main physiological aspect of the human speech production system is the vocal tract shape. The vocal tract modifies the spectral content of an acoustic wave as it passes through it, thereby producing speech. Hence, it is common in speaker verification systems to make use of features derived only from the vocal tract. Using cepstral analysis, an utterance may be represented as a sequence of feature vectors. Utterances spoken by the same person but at different times result in similar yet a different sequence of feature vectors. The purpose of voice modeling is to build a model that captures these variations in the extracted set of features. Systems based on these principles have a high level of accuracy and have been used for acess control purposes.

Multimodal Biometric System

A biometric system which relies only on a single biometric identifier in making a personal identification is often not able to meet the desired performance requirements. Identification based on multiple biometrics represents an emerging trend. A multimodal biometric system, which integrates face recognition, fingerprint verification, and speaker verification in making a personal identification takes advantage of the capabilities of each individual biometric. It can be used to overcome some of the limitations of a single biometrics. Preliminary experimental results demonstrate that the identity established by such an integrated system is more reliable than the identity established by a face recognition system, a fingerprint verification system, and a speaker verification system.

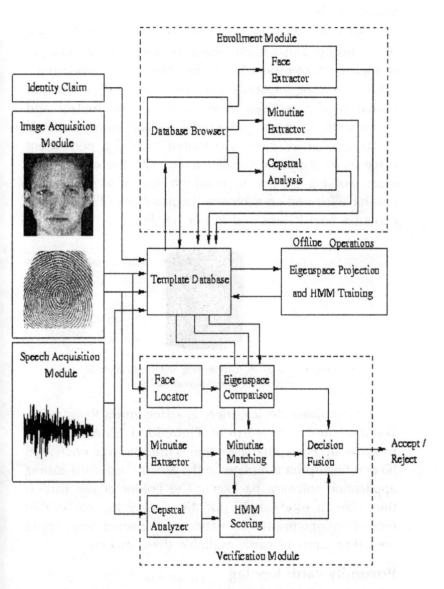

A Multi modal biometric system, employee's biometric details are taken at the enrollment stage and then verified at access points.
Courtesy: biometrics@cse.msu.edu. Detailed information on the above systems available at this website.

Smart cards

These are likely to find extensive usage due to their sheer utility and effectiveness as a simplistic identity verification tool especially in the maritime environment . With increasing security measures, the ISPS code and similar legal directives to establish access control and backgrounds of crew/ port employees and identity related databases, 'smart' cards are touted to find a permanent place in most people's wallet along with the credit card. Most working groups on maritime scurity in the recent past have focused on exploring the possibility of using smart cards on board ships and in port facilities.

an example of a smart card writing and verification device; see
http://www.ohanainternational.com

In the above device, there is a Fingerprint Registration Terminal and a Fingerprint Embedded SMART CARD program kit. Encryption algorithm is used to write encrypted ID and fingerprint template on the Smart Card (card issuing application software package). The holder of the card is thus able to establish his identity using the embedded biometric(fingerprint) information on the smart card. There are other kinds of cards available these include:

Proximity card/ Key tag

These are highly durable credit card sized proximity cards with any combination available with magnetic stripe and IC chip. Customized formats are available with these cards.

Easy to carry proximity cards for access control and attendance
see http://www.ohanainternational.com

Long Range Active Card

With a reading range upto 2.1m or more, this active card consists of a self contained battery, low battery signal transmit - 3~5 years battery life time (10 Times reading per day) ,User's Unique Format and ID number Programmable and other features. This saves time and convenience by actively operating at distances.

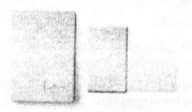

Active cards for access control and attendance
see http://www.ohanainternational.com

Application of biometrics in the marine environment
The Massport test

At Boston's logan International airpot (Massport), software from Minnesotta based Identix and Massachussets based Visage played a key role in trials intended to improve security in the wake of 9-11.

In this experiment Facial recognition was used as the 'active observer' who knew all the 250 faces of a 'hit list' and was able to read the crowd as it passed in front of its cameras. Finally it was able to spot a 'known' person 153 times but missed 93 times. Tests have shown that an average person is able to accurately match a 2- D representation (photograph) of a strangers face with a live image less than 70 % of the time- a result that is not significantly better than that achieved by massport FR technology. Technology since then has progressed, and soon itll be possible to achieve higher probabilities of 1:n recognition capabilities.High speed cameras and image processsing subsystems, RAM hosted databases, fast SMP software (i.e. multiple 64 bit CPUs and fast mother board busses) are available and advanced image labelling and cumulative match score decision rules could be created using current software technology. In addition if man in the loop attendant is taken into consideration who decides along with the software in difficult cases the probability of a hit rises significantly.

Applying biometrics

In general, biometric tecnhnologies can be applied in four broad application categories: Surveillance, screening, enrollment identification and identity verification. Not all biometric technologies are equally well suited to these purposes.

Surveillance applications rule out the possibility of using contact based biometrics data sensing, such as required by all fingerprint , signature, and hand geometry sensors. In addition all near contact biometric sensing techniques such as those employed by retina and iris image scan data capture are eliminated since these require a high degree of conscious cooperation by the subject whih may not be possible in hectic /or tourist environs of airports, ports and passenger vessels.

Basically, in this method after capturing the biometric image data, the match features contained in the data are coded and a one to many (1:n) search of an 'alert' database containing similarly coded biometric data from persons of interest is conducted.based on certain predetermined decision rules (eg. highest match score, the difference between the first and second candidate's score, a match score above a threshold, etc.) the system returns a result to the operator typically in the form of "probable match with candidate xxxx" or " no match".

Screening applications are similar to surveillance except that the environment is more constrained. Typical screening applications observe subjects as they pass through a portal that admits only a single person at a time. Screening applications employ the same 1:n match operation as described for surveillance. Random factors which need to be negotiated in surveillance techniques do not play a role in screening.

Enrollment identification services are characterised by overt biometric data collection, cooperative subjects and a rigidly controlled imaging environment. There is a need to extensively establish the background of the subject and give him a tamper-proof identity and a biometric data 'signature' in all major organisations and this is especially applicable in the marine environment; thus workers in ports and ship's crew background/id can now be established using this technology.

Enrollment applications employ the same 1:n match operations described for surveillance and screening except that the search is typically carried out not only against the 'alert' file, but also against the entire database of previously enrolled subjects. (in order to eliminate the possibility of of an individual obtaining more than one authorised identity using an alias.)

Identity verification applications are characterised by overt biometric data collection, cooperative subjects and a rigidly controlled imaging environment. Since the objective of the identity verification procedure is to verify the veracity of the subjects claim to a particular identity and the rights/ privileges authorised to that identity, the subject will be motivated and cooperative. After biometric data capture, the match features contained in the data are coded and a 1:1 search of a specific file containing similarly coded biometric data collected from the subject during his/her enrollment in to the system is conducted.

A binary result , typically 'match' or 'no match' is returned to the operator and the application then applies whatever steps are necessary verify the the subject's current authority to provide access to physical or logical assets, entry into secured perimeters etc. The ISPS code has stressed upon effective access control and monitoring and surveillance activities for both port facilities and vessels, thus utilisation of biometric technologies based on the principles listed above promises to be an effective and futuristic security solution. Creative utilisation of these technologies are obviously seen to meet security demands of a multitude of environments- these can be easily extended to the operational marine environment. Take for example, a security firms vision of securing elevators using smart card technology:

There are several aspects of "control". First, you can define when specific floors of specific elevators are to be in secure mode. Secondly, you can define cards so that only specific cards have access to specific floors when those floors are in secure mode. Further, you can define the cards to have access only during certain times. Lastly, if necessary, you can differentiate between one elevator and another, so that securing floors and accessibility can be performed on an individual elevator basis. Other systems may be quite complex with express elevators, multiple rises, multiple buildings, and the need to differentiate between the 10th floor of one elevator where the cafeteria is, and the 10th floor of a different elevator where the CEO's executive suite is.

This can easily be extended onto a marine application say a passenger vessel. Another example outlying security level flexibility is given by Ohana International:

Security Levels

1st Level : PIN Only
- Basic Access Control
- 4 to 6 digit PIN

2nd Level : Card + Password
- Double Check Access Control
- Combination of Card + Password

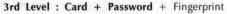

3rd Level : Card + Password + Fingerprint
- Triple Check Access Control
- Fast Verification [1 second]
- 1:1 Personal Identification

4th Level : Card + Password + Fingerprint + Face Recognition
- Multiple Modal High-End Security Access Control
- Fingerprint + Face Algorithm
- 1:1 Personal Identification

5th Level : Card +Password + Fingerprint + Face Recognition +Speaker Recognition
- Multiple Modal High-End Security Access Control
- Fingerprint + Face Algorithm
- 1:1 Personal Identification

In a model designed for airports, Imagis Technologies painted the following scenario (based on test figures of 99% accuracy for enrollment identification technologies achieved by modern biometric systems such as automated fingerprint identification systems operating against databases of millions of subjects and other current technology performance figures)

If 100 terrorists enter an air port where security is controlled by a layered area model, the probability that they will make it successfully through the security process, avoid detection, board an aircraft is as follows:

* 2 in 5 spotted in crowd before check in (surveillance)
* 99 % percent of 40 - identified during check in (screening)
* thus number of terrorists who will attempt to enter the security securing area= 0.4 while the probability of a terrorist escaping detection is 0 after security screening without FR surveillance the final number of terrorists entering this area was 1.

Behind the success of this model would be the application of all the above biometric principles and solutions available today at an extensive scale. Steps should be taken to employ these initiatives in the marine environment too. Thus biometrics today offers maximum promise for use in ports and ships.

These technological aids will boost the modern security initiative. Existing technologies such as X-Ray back scatter containers portals (for detection of drugs, weapons etc.), advanced traffic mangement systems, satellite communications have been highly successful in revamping old methodologies - to an extent which can be termed revolutionary. The above outlined technologies could very well be part of the next generation of the technology resource multiplication wave, hitting the maritime security environment as well. Implementation of thse and other new technologies is highly recommended.

Epilogue:
Crystal Gazing

The Mega Trend Towards The Oceans

The 21st Century will be the century when mankind increasingly takes to the sea. Issues like global warming and the rising curve of the worlds population will put increasing pressure upon the fragile ecosystems of the earths land areas and severely tax their resources. Mankind will have to increasingly look towards the oceans to supplement its sources of food, nourishment, metals and minerals. Offshore oil is already meeting a fair percentage of mankind's energy needs. Polymetallic Nodules and deep sea mining may be needed to meet the world economies increasing appetite for resources and energy. In the far future, we may have floating cities and harbours and habitations on the Sea. Instead of reaching out to outer space, and the distant stars and planets – mankind may well have to reach out first for the inner spaces of the Oceans of Planet Earth itself in its search for a new lebensaraum.

Today, we do not have the open spaces of uncharted continents in America and Australia to act as a migration safety net for absorbing the doubling and tripling of the worlds population. The only space available to mankind is either outer space-travel to other planets and galaxies or a migration to the inner space of the oceans and the seas of the earth itself..

According to World Bank estimates, in 1999, the world sea borne trade was pegged at 21,480 billion ton-miles. It is expected to touch 35,000 billion ton miles in 2010 and 41,800 billion ton miles in 2014. This implies a veritable doubling of the global sea borne trade. The United Nations Conference on Trade and Development (UNCTAD) in its report on "Review of Maritime Transport 2000", noted that world sea borne trade recorded its 14th consecutive annual increase and Asia's share of imports and exports was 26.1 and 18.8 percent respectively. Clearly mankind is headed for the High Seas in a big way. If that is so, issues of maritime security will assume much greater importance and salience. Today, our Sea Lanes of Communications (SLOCs) are being threatened from a number of directions.

The Eagle has landed

9/11 are numerals that have etched themselves in the collective consciousness of the world. As the world has globalised so too the threats it faces have become global and widespread. The new threat is from irrational non-state actors bent upon wreaking mindless havoc and destruction. These destructive elements played havoc with the aviation industry in September 2001. In a macabre twist to earlier hijacking plots, the terrorists used aviation fuel laden airliners as cruise missiles to target Americas key institutions of high symbolic value. They struck the Continental United States in a very comprehensive and meticulously planned manner and extracted a massive toll in lives and property.

The Fifth Horseman: The Onset of Mega Terror

The lessons of the hit that the aviation industry took then are food for thought for the shipping industry today. Security norms have been traditionally much more stringent in the Aviation industry than in the maritime trade. The prevalence of Maritime Crime in fields such as Flags of Convenience, Phantom Ships, Stealing of Cargoes etc. creates a very fertile situation tailor made for exploitation by Global Terrorist Organisations. Maritime crime in fact forms the very vulnerable flank of sea borne commerce and may constitute the thin edge that will invite the wedge of Mega terror events on the high seas. The global war on terror is far from over. The Al Qaida has been hit and disrupted but it has not been destroyed.

Osama Bin Laden had formed the International Islamic Front (IIF) in 1998. This was a vast alliance of Jehadi Terrorist Organisations which include:-

- 5 Organisations in Pakistan.
- Al Qaida and Taliban in Afghanistan.
- Two Organisations in Central Asia.
- Three Groups from Egypt.
- Abbu Sayaff and Free Acheh Movement in Philippines and Indonesia.

So far only the Afghanistan based groups have been disrupted along with some of the Central Asian Organisations. All the other groups are fully intact and have demonstrated their efficacy and lethality by the Bali and Madrid bombings and the other recent incidents. An Egyptian air liner with some 140 French tourist crashed lately. Some terrorist organisations have claimed responsibility. There have been a number of terror bombings in Saudi Arabia and Pakistan itself as also in Turkey (Istanbul), Casablanca, Iraq and in Madrid (Spain).

There are palpable signs of regrouping and revival. The current volatile situation in Iraq and Palestine is bound to add to the ranks of the *Jehadis*. What is of much graver concern is the growing convergence of the phenomena of piracy and terrorism and its linkages with maritime crime. A number of plausible scenarios have been sketched in the First Chapter of this book to show how Mega Terror could next manifest on and from the high seas. Almost two decades ago a very perceptive piece of fiction had shown the Fifth Horseman of the Apocalypse landing on the American shore in a Cargo Container. He was armed with a suitcase nuclear bomb. Today, he is more likely to use a simpler Radiological Dispersal Device (RDD). Media reports indicate that two senior Pakistani Nuclear Scientists (Bashirudin Ahmed and Sultan Mehmood) had met Osama Bin Laden on a number of occasions and may well have provided adequate instruction for assembling such an RDD to his cohorts. Weapons of Mass Destruction in the hands of such non-state actors constitute the most serious threat to the existing order of nation states in the years to come. The arena of the global war against terrorism may well be shifting to the high seas. Bin Laden is rumoured to have a Phantom fleet of some 20 odd ships under Flags of Convenience. The growing convergence of the phenomena of piracy and terrorism in the Muslim populations of Indonesia and Philippines becomes cause for serious disquiet when we juxtapose the fact that a large proportion of the crews for the worlds merchant fleets are recruited from these states.

Need to Equate Piracy with Terrorism

There is a growing global awareness about the need to equate piracy with terrorism. The apparent distinction between the two phenomena are purely illusory. The

International Maritime Bureau has strongly advocated such an equation. Piratic attacks are armed and invariably result in the inhuman murder of crews or callously setting them adrift. These pose a direct threat to the worlds lifelines of economy and trade. There is an urgent need to include piracy in the ambit of terrorism and bring it within the scope of the global war against terror. This is an urgent imperative.

Summary of Threats and Anticipatory Responses

A reactive outlook that waits for a disaster to happen before responding to it, could prove to be catastrophic. The shipping industry will have to ingest many lessons from the Aviation Industry's travails at the hands of terrorists. It will have to anticipate events and threats and act in a proactive manner to stave them off and plug all loopholes before these are exploited. The Terrorist threat on the high seas is not a piece of fiction or mere hyperbole. Osama Bin Laden had sent his nephew Mohammad Jama Khalifa to the Philippines to subvert the Muslim youth of that nation. Reportedly a number of training camps have been set up.

Indonesia and the Philippines are two island nations with a growing seafaring tradition. In fact today they supply a huge proportion of crews for the worlds shipping fleets. It is pertinent therefore to note the design of the fundamentalist terrorist organisation in these states

- **The Moro Islamic Liberation Front** This is a 12,500 strong rebel group that has been fighting for the past 25 years against the Philippines Govt. It is only now that the struggle has been hijacked in the past few years by fundamentalist elements. The Moro group is based in the Southern Philippine Islands of Mindanao. A number of training camps have been set up and the violent activities of these group are on the rise steadily. One of the most prominent terrorist groups is the Abu Sayaff Group which has been responsible for a large number of recent bombing incidents and terrorists attacks.

- **The Free Acheh Movement (GAM)** The Free Acheh Movement of Indonesia is another ongoing Islamic insurgency that has strong fundamentalist linkages. It is spread over the old tract of the Sri Vijaya kingdom. The Jamait-I-Islami mentors of this movement have been trained in Pakistan and Afghanistan. It has focused on a series of bomb attacks in Bali and other high profile targets in Indonesia. The Indonesian paratroopers recently launched major operations against this rebel groups.

Yemen: Recent terrorist strikes on the sea have mostly originated from Yemen. There have been the high profile attacks on the *USS Cole* (American Destroyer) and the French oil tanker *MT Limburg*. An Islamic group called the Army of Aden claimed responsibility for both these attacks. Reportedly it is closely linked to the Al Qaida. This remains a high threat area.

Somalia: Somalia is a classic failed State which becomes a shatter zone of collapse. Such zones are ideal for breeding and sustaining terrorist movements. In Somalia today, there is no Central Government authority and warlord factions are perpetually at war with themselves. A number of incidents of piracy have taken place in and around the Somali coastal waters (including abortive attacks with RPG-7 Rocket Launchers)

Sri Lanka: The ongoing civil war in this country has taken a toll of over 60,000 killed. The LTTE is an extremely well organised terrorist group that is deeply involved in smuggling, narcotics trade and extensive gun running in the region. This is a terrorist group with a strong maritime orientation. It has a Naval Arm called Sea Tigers which has attacked and sunk a number of Sri Lankan Naval vessels on the Sea and in Sri Lankan coastal waters. It has a fleet of 10-12 freighters. As stated earlier, a Sri Lankan rebel group had attempted to take over the Island nation of Maldives in 1990.

Pakistan: Pakistan's ISI had set up the Taliban regime in Afghanistan. There were just 275 Madrasas in Pakistan in 1947. today the number of registered Madrassas alone has gone up to 11,000. If we include the unregistered ones the number goes upto 45,000. The Wahabi Madrassas on the Pak-Afghan border are the prime hub centers for terrorism and constitute a Jihad Factory that turns out thousands of recruits for the global *Jihad* every year. These Madrassas have armed and trained a huge number of Islamic warriors of a global *Jihad* who have been fighting in Kashmir, Chechnya, Bosnia, Central Asian Republics and lately even in Iraq. Currently however, the Pakistani govt has executed a U Turn in these policies and has been pressurised to join the US Global war against terror. However, fundamentalist influence is still strong in the middle and lower ranks of the Pakistani Armed Forces and the ISI. It has been supporting Islamic terrorist groups active in India and provides them explosives and arms through smuggling via the sea route. It has also been trying to bolster fundamentalist terrorist/*Jehad* organizations in Bangladesh and Nepal.

These are the prime/high threat areas that must be considered into all plans for ensuring maritime security and the safety of ships and sea borne commerce, as also the security of our ports and harbours. Threats to global sea borne commerce could originate from these regions and all nation states will have to act in concert to ensure the safety of the global SLOCs. The Shipping industry will have to consciously review its routing options to steer clear of such zones. It must also insist on Naval patrolling of sensitive SLOCs and choke points, preferably under UN auspices. The ISPS Code is a major and timely initiative, that all countries in the world must do their best to promote and thereby further enhance the Safety of Life at Sea. Legislation is one aspect. Ensuring these are enforced is even more important. Mankind's destiny in the 21st century lies in the sea. We will have to make these safe for sea borne commerce, for energy extraction, deep sea mining and sea bed farming.

Technology Initiatives and Global Solutions

Global threats call for global solutions. This is where we need to anticipate threats and turn to Technology in a major way to ensure the safety of our maritime fleets, our sea borne commerce and our SLOCs. Information Technology and Space Based sensors hold the key to the future of Security on the High Seas. At the conclusion of this book one would like to summarize and highlight some of the technological solutions being explored today.

Information Technology Applications

ECDIS: It is note-worthy that as early as 1995, Electronic Chart Display and Information System (ECDIS) has been accepted as a substitute for paper nautical charts. The IMO set up performance standards for ECDIS in that year.

RCDS: These also cover Raster based Chart Display Systems. Both of these are Geographical Information Systems that are replacing paper nautical charts even as rasterised maps are fast replacing surveyed maps on land.

EPFS/GPS: The next evolutionary step from ECDIS and RCDS is Electronic Position Fixing System or EPFS. This is another term for the Global Positioning System (GPS) which is based on the existing Global Navigation Satellite System. GPS fixes of the ships location can be received by Global Satellite Receivers on board the ship. These will increasingly make Radio Direction Finders totally obsolete. In advanced Western Armies, Air Forces and the Navies the bulk of the Navigation is now almost entirely based upon GPS. Currently, the maritime fleets are in the process of transition from routine nautical charts and tables to the GPS mode. ECDIS and RCDS may only be used currently if there is adequate back up arrangement in terms of nautical charts and publications. Reliance on the GPS has grown by leaps and bounds already and the Maritime Industry today incorporates this position fixing method in all technological and security initiatives. The GPS in however a US Department of Defence enterprise and is not independent of their control.

The civil industry's answer to the military controlled GPS is the Galileo project. Sponsored by the European Union, the project will reach a state of readiness by 2008 and will likely to be universally adoped by the Maritime Industry. India has a stake in this futuristic system of accurate satellite position fixing.

Integrated Bridge Systems: With the advancements in ECDIS & Ships steering control, the INS (Integrated Navigation Systems) has come into existence. It is likely to consist of a Navigation module, anti-collision module and steering control module. The INS is thus able to plan a passage and monitor the vessels movement, alter courses in collision situations and at waypoints of the same plan. It is regarded as an important part of full ship automation system with interface being provided for data exchange.

Integrated Bridge Systems: IBS is basically a combination of INS and other ship board systems aimed at increasing the safe and efficient management of a ship.

As per IMO the IBS should include the following.

a) Passage Execution

b) Communication

c) Machinery Control

d) Loading and discharging and cargo control.

e) Safety and Security

With advanced Navigation equipments, motion sensor cameras, modern equipment like VDR, AIS, CCTV systems, microprocessor being integrated; the stage is set for fully automated management of the vessel as well as vessels security. Japan has already experimented with an unmanned vessel making a high seas voyage. An independent microprocessor ordering the vessel to evade a small boat, or presenting a non lethal shock to an intruder-could be tomorrow's reality.

Automatic Ship Identification System: As has been stated earlier, ship based transponders are being introduced in the entire mercantile fleets of the world in a phased manner between 01 Jul 2002 to 01Jul 2008. These must be capable of ship to ship and ship to shore information exchange and must provide ships the following data :-

• Identity and type.

• Position.

• Course, Speed and Navigation Status.

• Other Safety related Information.

Brian Ring of the Japanese Radio Company (UK) has stated that AIS should be preferably used with RADAR not ECIDS and it should never be used solely on its own.

Voyage Data Recorders: These are the equivalent of the Black Boxes being used currently on the airliners of the civil aviation industry. This is a prime requirement in the context of piracy and terrorism threats on the sea. The SOLAS amendments to the Vth Chapter of the SOLAS have already made it mandatory for all passenger ships. Existing ro-ro passenger ships in fact were required to retrofit by 01 Jul 2002. All other passenger ships are required to retrofit by 01 Jul 2004. This is based on the higher level of terrorist threats to passenger ships (based upon an analysis of the profile of terrorist attacks encountered so far.)

Long Range Ship Identification and Tracking: The most critical technological force multiplier against threats of piracy, hijacking and terrorist attacks is the long range identification and tracking of ships. The IMO has acknowledged that Inmarsat polling is currently an appropriate system for such long range identification and polling of ships and has urged all contracting Governments to urgently install such systems on all ships.

Networked Solutions of the Future: Network Centric warfare is the buzz word of the future. As far as the shipping industry is concerned it will also need to network all ship board computers of the merchant fleets on to a global mercantile internet. The author envisages such a networked solution to the current threats being faced by merchant vessels on the high seas. This would involve a networking of all ship based computers so that the moment another ship is detected by RADAR and queried/polled by own ship based transponders, the entire ship data is displayed on ECDIS. If a vessel is not immediately identified by the ship based computer data base, the merchant vessel should take early avoidance measures/evasive action to prevent/obviate coming in the proximity of the ship. Such unidentified contact must also be reported to shore and the Piracy Center. The key here is systems integration and the establishment of a Maritime Internet Facility for Security. All ships in the near future will be equipped with AIS (Automatic Identification System) transponders. These should be integrated with the existing ECDIS (Electronic Chart Display and Information Systems). This would in turn be integrated with a host of navigation systems like the ARPA, Gyro etc. The key to enhancement of response capabilities would lie in data fusion systems. In effect this would mean that the moment we encounter traffic in the future, instead of scurrying from the chart room to the RADAR, ARPA and the VHF to establish contact with the approaching vessel, to carry out an appraisal of her intention – one would simply need to click upon the target ship on the ECDIS display. This would open a data window giving full details of the target – including her name/call sign/IMO number, her route information, speed, course and even her manoeuvring intention would be flashed. The manoeuvring intent could be automatic, say – a major alteration on the gyro-reading would be detected and transmitted as "Altering course to port" to all vessels in the vicinity via the AIS. The spin offs for navigation are evident. For security, we could have a " situation avoidance rule" for ships with suspicious/ no identification. In sensitive areas even crew ID numbers could be transmitted. On query their security background checked clearance could be flashed on Information windows in the ECDIS consoles. Suspicious craft could thereby be given wide berth well in advance. Can we bring the plethora of crafts plying the ocean and seas under scrutiny and surveillance? That is the security challenge of the coming decades. It is note worthy that e-mail is already replacing the traditional Fax as a means of ship to shore communication e-mail enables the following:-

- Container strorage planning centre provide prestow information that enables the ships to make ballast water adjustments prior to port arrival.

- Ship agents receive crew lists and even digital photographs and biometric information via e-mail which speeds up port administration.

- Digital Photographs can enhance repair lists.

- Fuel Analysis reports and bunkers could be delt with by e-mail

- Weather routing software onships can be up dated by e-mail data.

- Schedules and crew relief arrangements can now be arranged by e-mail.

- Lastly there are personal e-mails sent and received by crew members.

- Daily news sheets and security information can also beent via e-mail to ships.

- The current network operating system is windows NT based and the current workstations are pentium PCs. Currently access to the world wide web is not available and only the e-mail part of it is available to ships.

- On board systems today provide high quality two way direct dial fax, telex, e-mail and data communication to and from almost anywhere on the world.

Ergonomics of Bridge Design and Display: With the increasing impact and exploitation of Information Technology for Navigation and Ship Tracking and Identification, the human factor will have to be incorporated in terms of changes in the Ergonomics of the bridge design and the design and arrangements of new systems and equipment. Currently in most existing bridges, the personal working on the Nautical Charts have their back to the ARPA/ECDIS display screens. The Chart table could be so aligned that those operating on them face front so as to concurrently be able to see the ARPA and the visual arc forward. ECIDS should also be located in the front portion (so as to be aligned to the direction of ship movement) and permit concurrent viewing of the forward zone, the ARPA panel ECIDS. This calls for an ergonomic redesign of the Bridge perse and the installation of totally comprehensive bridge systems.

Voyage Planning: There will also be a greater need for more meticulous Voyage Planning to avoid/bypass threatened sectors of the route and avoid dangerous situations. It is here that networked solutions will help and mid course corrections could be applied in real time as any fresh incident of piracy, hijacking or terrorist attack takes place. Alerts could be put out on the mercantile internet and would automatically flash on the ECDIS screens of all ships in the vicinity—advising them to alter course/take evasive action or come to the rescue for SAR purposes.

The writing therefore, is on the wall. The 21st Century will be the century of the sea. To that extent security at sea will be a global concern that will call for global solutions. Information Technology can be a prime tool towards that end. The threats are palpable and real and must be responded to urgently. All nation states will have to coordinate their responses and devise global solutions as have been envisaged in the ISPS Code and allied amendments to the SOLAS Convention. What is at stake is a huge and growing vulnerability of some 46,000 merchant ships and over 4000 ports. It is a huge vulnerability. Any strike on maritime commerce could deal a mortal blow to the fragile global economy and bring it crashing down in a matter of days. A mega terror strike on US ports itself can impose costs of 58 billion dollars in a day. The impact of global disruption will be far worse than the local destruction caused. Where WMDs are employed the impact can be truly catastrophic.

References

Books

1. Ahmed Rashid "The Resurgence of Central Asia : Islam or Nationalism". Oxford University Press Karachi 1994.

2. *Ibid.* "Taliban : Islam, Oil and the New Great Game in Central Asia". IB Tarus Publishers. London. 2001 Reprint.

3. Brig. G D Bakshi SM,VSM "Afghanistan : The First Fault Line War", Lancer Publishers. New Delhi. Revised Ed. 2002.

4. Gurr Cole Benjamin "The New Face of Global Terrorism" 2003.

5. Onwudieve Ihekwoaba. D. "The Globalisation of Terrorism" 2001.

6. KPS Gill and Ajay Sahni "The Global Threat of Terror" 2002.

7. Rahul Roy Choudhury "India's Maritime Security" *Knowledge World*. New Delhi. Jun 2000.

8. Rohan Gunaratna "Inside Al Qaida Global Network of Terror" 2002.

9. Janes "Infantry Weapons"

10. US Maritime Transport Committee Report of Jul 2003 (Prepared for Organisation for Economic Cooperation and Development).

Articles/Papers

1. Aline De Bivere "Solas Takes a New Track" *Ocean Voice*. Apr 2001.

2. Ashok Malik and Lavina Melwani "Sixty Minutes" Article in *India Today*. 24 Sep 2001.

3. A K Verma "Identifying the Nature of Current Terrorism : What its Containment Requires". *Indian Defence Review*. Vol. 18 (1) dt Jan-Mar 2003.

4. Doyle M C Manus Report Published in *Times of India* 10 Oct. 2001.

5. Evan Thomas *et al* "Road to 11 September" *Article in News Week* 01 Oct 2001.

6. Thomas.E. Ricks. Report published in *Times of India* 10 Oct 2001.

7. Stefan Leader "Osama Bin Laden's Quest for Weapons of Mass Destruction" *Janes Intelligence Review*. Jun 1994.

8. Lt Cdr R.C. Browbick "Piracy : Ancient Myth or Modern Reality" *Naval Review*. Feb 2003, Vol. 91. No 1.

9. Carl Conetta "Terrorism, World Order and Co-operative Security. Review of International Affairs" No 1107. Jul-Sep 2002.

10. Matin Zuberi "Nuclear Terrorism : High Risk, Low Probability". *Aakrosh*. Jan 2003. Vol.6. No 18.

11. Bharat Karnad "Facing Pre-emption and an Emerging Adverse Scenario in the Indian Ocean Region". *Trishul* Vol. XV No. 2.

12. Vice Admiral Premvir Das "Maritime Terrorism : Piracy at Sea" *Military Yearbook 2003-04*.

13. Vijay Sakhuja : "Indian Ocean and the Safety of Sea Lines of Communication". *Strategic Analysis* Vol XXV No 5. Aug 2001.

14. Philip Day "Ship Piracy Stirs Terrorism Fears" *Wall Street Journal* Fri/Sat/Sunday Jun 13-15, 2003.

15. Vice Admiral (retd) G M Hiranandani "Patrolling the Indian Ocean" *Indian Defence Review* Apr-Jun 2003. Vol 18 (2).

Internet

1. Operation Safe Commerce . httpill uvw.dhs.gov/display. www.itsa:org.

2. What are Flags of Convenience. A brief guide to Flags of Convenience. www. ltf. Og uk/seafarer/foe/Body foc.html.

3. IMB Calls for Clamp down on fake Maritime Documents . www. Iccwbo. Org/ccs/news archives/ 2001/imb fakes.asp.

4. Murky Flags of Convenience, Ship Registry System Could hamper effort to Uncover Terrorist Assetts". www.amo-union.org/Newspaper/morgue/11-2001/ section/mews/foc.html.

5. Rahul Roy Choudhury "US Naval Policy in the Indian Ocean" http:ll www.idsa-india,org/an-dec8-4.html.

6. Rahul Bedi. US Increases Naval Presence in Indian Ocean. *"South Asia Tribune"*. http:ll www. Satribune.com/archives/jan 13 1903/opinion. US bases.htm.

Index